Appelley Publishing

2020 RISING STARS COLLECTION

The Rising Stars Collection represents our student authors
as accurately as possible.
Every effort has been made to print each poem
as it was submitted with minimal editing
of spelling, grammar, and punctuation.
All submissions have been formatted to this compilation.

Copyright © 2020 by Appelley Publishing as a compilation.

Copyrights to individual poems belong to the authors.

All rights reserved.
No part of this book may be reproduced in any way
without the expressed written permission of the publisher.

Published by
Appelley Publishing
P.O. Box 582
Tarpon Springs, FL 34688
Website: www.appelley.org
Email: help@appelley.org

Printed in the United States of America.

Appelley
Publishing

ISBN: 978-1-7322140-2-6

CONTENTS

★★★★★★★★★

Foreword 4

Outstanding Participation Award 5

POETRY

Division I
Grades 3-5... 7

Division II
Grades 6-8 43

Division III
Grades 9-12.. 151

Index of Authors.. 202

Ordering the Collection.. 207

★★★★★★★★★

FOREWORD

Welcome to the Rising Stars Collection of Student Poetry.
If you're wondering what's on the minds of today's youth,
you're about to find out.
Within these pages are the hopes and heartaches,
triumphs and tragedies,
challenges and celebrations
they experience every day.
We consider it a privilege to bring them to you,
just as we all should consider it a responsibility to understand.
After all, their world is our world,
and their vision is our future.
To our student authors,
congratulations on a job well done.
You have shown great courage in sharing your lives with us,
and we want you to know that we're proud of you.

L. Sean James
Editor

2020 OUTSTANDING PARTICIPATION AWARD

MCCORD JUNIOR HIGH SCHOOL
SYLVANIA, OHIO

DIVISION I

GRADES 3–5

Rabbits
by Sophia Tambone

Rabbits are so cute
Happily hopping around
They will make you laugh

Books
by Crystal Clydesdale

Books
Smooth, addictive
Reading, imagining, learning
Full of words and adventures
Texts

The Wolf
by Claire Lyon

My howl is like the trees swaying in the wind.
I am as silent as the leaves falling from their branches.
The forest is my home, my palace, my kingdom.
I will rule it forever.

Autumn
by Emily Godek

The nice smell of apples, the colorful leaves,
I finally get to wear long sleeves.
Not too hot, not too cold.
Autumn is the perfect season, that never gets old.

Life In the Wild
by Isabella Horne

Pine trees bend in the wind
The smell of evergreen overpowers me
Pine needles all over the ground
As I stomp, they don't make a sound
Leaves of colors, red, yellow, and orange
All over the ground, making it disappear
Smelling pine and sap from every direction
Watching deer dart in and out of the woods
Catching fish is such a breeze
I love life in the wilderness.

Halloween
by Amelia Trejgis

Scary Halloween!
I like to trick or treat!
Who else does?

Ladybugs
by Annabella Hillegas

Some ladybugs fly on a flower
Some ladybugs fly on a tower
Some ladybugs fly on a ladder
All of these ladybugs live in a garden

Who Is the Wind?
by Alaina Jackson

Can you tell who is the wind?
Who is it?
The strong wind, the person that is the wind, that is who you are.
Are you supposed to do this?
Are you the good wind or are you the bad wind?

Planes
by Ajay Singh

Planes, planes;
They soar up high in the sky at super high speeds.
Planes, planes;
They can twirl and swirl and land far away as the imagination can see.
They see stuff that we dream of.

The Trees
by Sophia Rosero

The trees so tall in the sky.
So free, bright and green.
Nature's true beauty.
Some touch the clouds, others hover close to the ground.
Trees surround me everywhere.
Since the beginning of time ... they have been here.
Trees in the sky, woods and fields.
I would like to be a tree.
So lovely and free.

Mosquito
by Massimo Vachino

They bite;
It itches;
It's a problem,
but there are many other problems that are worse.
But soon it fades away.
Do not worry.
It's no longer a problem when they fly away.

My Story About Glasses
by Azi Jacob

When I got glasses, I thought I was so cool for having glasses
I didn't need to wear them full-time
But I still did because I thought I looked very cool
For wearing them full-time even though I didn't need to wear them
Somebody was making fun of me – he said that I didn't need to wear glasses
But I did need glasses
I just wore my glasses full-time
And then they got used to seeing me wear them full-time
and they didn't make fun of me ever again

My Little Furball
by Chava Rivka Roffman

I have a little guinea pig and Snowball is his name
You think he'd like to run a lot but he's just very lame
I feed him carrots every day but that's just not enough
He needs his pellets and his hay to keep him very stuffed
I clean his cage every week like it should be done
I spray it with some vinegar to get the odors gone
Every day when I come home I see his piercing eyes
I love to hold him close to me, he is my furry prize
So as you can see, my furball is as cute as can be

Shining Stars
by Jino Hartman-Vicinanza

The stars are shining like the sun in the dark night.
Wherever there's darkness there's also light.
Shining stars can be dimed but never put out.
Light will always shine through the darkness.
Light will never die even in the darkest hours.
in present, past, or the future light will still be stronger than darkness.
In our past God is the light and the serpent was the darkness
and now we know that the light will always be here to protect us.
And we are the children of the light and the next generation of new lights.

Wind
by George Siabanis

The way it sways;
The way it looks;
The way it makes you feel.
The way it characterizes you.
The breeze that's in your hair;
Life that it gives you.
The trees going back and forth.

The City
by Xavier Jonathan Osorio

Cats lurking in the shadows of an alley
People out of work dilly-dallying
The sound of car honks fill the air
Everywhere
People walking their dogs left and right
The sun shining oh so bright
Skyscrapers touching the clouds
On the first floor is such a crowd
This is the city

The Poem of the Darkness Night
by Mary Rose Kells

As I walk into the darkness of night
I hear dancing.
As I'm walking down the alley
As I hear the cars beeping up and down the street.
As the songs of the dance fill my ears
As the wind blows my face
I do a jig,
Why I sung that jig
is because I was scared.

Snowstorm
by Natalya Battisti

As I hear the rustle of the trees
All I see in the sky is a horse tail
and I know it is ready to snow.
All of a sudden I feel a snowflake on my head
and I don't hear any crickets, birds, or squirrels.
I know it is winter.
The first snowflake has fallen
In the morning I go outside and I hear the crunch
as I step on the solid snow that is sparkly and shiny snow.

You Are Worth It
by Julia Potts

You are enough.
You are worth it.
You are brilliant like a shining star.
You can do it!
You are okay and loved.
You will be okay, I promise.
Don't be sad.
Believe in yourself.
Don't listen to them.
You are beautiful ...
It's okay to be different.
Reassure yourself-
The way you talk, like soft angels singing.
The way you walk, like gliding on water.
You are strong!
You are one in seven billion ...
YOU ARE WORTH IT.

Man In The Moon
by Kanisha Shiv

When the man in the moon looks down, he frowns in pain
How could a tiny little world be so vain
A world that is blue and green, one that is thought to be clean
But instead, makes a scene, the man in the moon
Watches little human hands, burn down lands
Little human brains, that create hurricanes
Little human eyes, that speak lies
Little human mouths, that always pout
Little human noses, that no more smell roses
He watches a little world turn insane
He knows it won't be long, till that planet burns down
He knows it won't be long, till we're all gone
But, he will be wrong
Out of nowhere will come a dawn of hope
little miracles will be born from the slope
They will plant flowers and mindful towers
They will bring the world to peace and ease, the world shall fall to its knees
The little miracles will take broken hands and create lands
They will wash away brains that create hurricanes
They once again will makes us see colors
They will make little noses once again smell roses
They will make mouths talk it out
They once again makes Earth feel like its worth
They will make humans see that all for one is worth
Then the man in the moon will look down and smile
To see that he was wrong all along

Math Is an Amazing Path
by Aidan Lambrianidis

Math is my favorite subject.
It's as simple as that.
We learn about 3D shapes.
They never look flat.
Even when math can be difficult.
It can also be fun.
You can learn about telling time.
And tell the time for everyone.
We learn about powers of ten.
It's so easy and fun.
That I don't want it to end.
As you can see, you learn a lot in math.
Though it is a long way.
It's a giant learning path.
Though ELA and grammar are about putting words together.
Math is mainly about numbers and making them bigger and better.
Even when people may say that recess is better than the rest.
In my head I will always say.
"Math will always be the best."

Autumn
by Mairaa Haiyder

Oh autumn, oh autumn, so sweet and delicious.
The season after summer. Should I talk about sweet food or beautiful weather?
Allow me to start with the weather.
As I walk through the leaves they are crunching,
they are on top of cars, on the ground, and some are still on trees.
The leaves turn red, yellow, brown, or orange but then there are the evergreens.
Autumn's light cool breeze blows by my face.
It brings different emotions to people
like sadness, happiness, excitement, etc.
In autumn, nights get longer and the days get shorter.
Oh, who cares if we get less sleep, we have to eat.
Autumn's seasonal food is very delicious and sweet.
Drinks are filled with pumpkin spice, cinnamon, or whip cream as a little treat.
Foods or drinks like pie, lattes, frappuccinos, cake pops, muffins,
and donuts have all those flavors. Pumpkin and apple picking are in season.
Go fast, get yours before they run out!
Halloween is coming, better have your costume planned out!
Children are knocking doors for sweets.
You'll see and hear vampires and zombies saying, "Trick or treat."
Now October is over, autumn is almost over, it's November now,
Thanksgiving is here! We are all eating turkey, mashed potatoes, and more,
The yummy tastes of all the food, but wait,
for autumn is over, winter has begun.
See you next year autumn!

Fall
by Charles Nugent

Leaves fall to the ground
Playing in the leaves is fun!
Temperatures go down

My 1,000 Pets
by Sarah Wang

I have 1,000 pets. Yes, I know it may sound crazy.
It all started in a little town with a woman named Daisy.
Daisy was the person who gave me all 1,000 pets,
and that is why I have 46 ferrets.
I have 4 lions, 1 tiger, a moose, and 16 pigs.
I have 17 hamsters and 100 zebras who like to eat figs.
There are 64 birds and 72 skunks and 13 fish that say "blub".
I have 2 baby elephants, 14 bunnies,
and 3 mice that like to swim in the tub.
I have 51 deer plus 7 cats, 2 giraffes, 6 dogs, and 14 rats.
I have 24 cows and 42 sheep,
18 chickens with 4 chicks that say "peep!"
I have a lizard and a hermit crab, a guinea pig and an owl,
a spider and a hedgehog and a wolf that likes to howl.
There are many, many others. So many I can't tell you.
I hope you enjoyed my poem,
and I hope you write one too.

Kindness Counts
by Lanabelle Messina

Has there ever been a day,
Where you just didn't know what to say?
When you felt sort of sad,
Or got kind of mad?
When you didn't quite fit in,
Not knowing how or when.
Have your friends left you out,
When all you do is pout?
Can you feel yourself get strong,
When it's in you all along?!
Even though it's hard,
You can let down your guard.
Because what you do,
Comes back to you-
What you may just find,
Is somebody who is kind.
Look for a life-long friend,
Who is sweet until the end.

Deer
by Macy Angstadt

Deer have a great fear of humans
so they make sure it's clear before going out in open
so hunters are nowhere near so the deer slowly creep out
and if they hear a peep they leap out of sight
and come back at night!

The Strong Girl In Hiding
by Liana M. Lall

The sky darkened, and the clouds thickened.
She tried to find her way around, but she couldn't.
Everyone told her,
That she wouldn't.
She was too young to win games.
At least that's what people thought.
They always had to make teams.
Still, she fought, and fought, and fought.
She knew her day would come soon.
Someday, from somewhere.
Where she could beat them all.
Where she didn't have to hold her breath, she could take to the air.
The sky lit up now,
And she had a great day
She didn't look down once,
And she didn't fear days away.

My Best Friend
by Daniel Schumacher, Jr.

I have a friend and he makes me smile, even when he drives me wild.
We have fun when we run up and down the hill,
I remember once I even took a spill.
He snores sometimes which makes me laugh but I hate when he passes gas.
My best friend is always around for me, when I am down he lifts me up.
He can be as quiet as a mouse or so loud I can't think
but either way I am glad he doesn't stink.
I see him morning, noon, and night and we will always be super tight.
Our friendship will never bend because we will be together until the end.
Can't you see, we are simply meant to be? But please don't be so serious,
just because you're curious to see who this amazing friend can be.
Well come on by, because you see my best friend lives with me.
If you are still in the dark and can't figure it out, here is one final clue.
My best friend tends to bark if he doesn't know you.
He never bites but he does give people a fright cause he's as big as me.
My best friend was a furry friend in need
until he came home to be with my family.

The Forest
by Amanda Inzerillo

All the leaves surround me.
Leaves on the ground, hear them rustle.
Rivers flowing calm and free.
Through the night the animals sleep.
Hear all the calming sounds.
Now it's only the forest and me.

Dance Is Extraordinary
by Charlotte Tone

I love to dance,
It's so much fun!
Especially with my friends,
'cause they're all a home run!
My skills might take time,
And some can be hard.
All you do is practice,
All out in the yard.
My favorite tricks are,
Back tucks and turns.
They are very fun to do,
If you have any concerns.
But this is just a dream,
You silly, sleepy head.
So go pursue that dream,
And get up out of bed.

The Perfect Pizza
by Brodie Latimer

My purple, radioactive, perilous, petrifying pizza
With pickles and pepperoni and plums and pears and pies and pineapples
Tasted good but remember, it was radioactive.
I turned into a cyclops, ugly as can be.
With one eye and pizza thighs, I put away my pizza.
The toppings jumped at me.
They were vicious and strong but I managed to eat them.
They tasted good, really good, but then I started feeling dizzy.
I said, "Oh no, I'm feeling dizzy again?!"
Waagghh.
When I woke up again, the pizza had wings!
It flew at me, hit me in the face and then I realized
it wanted to be my friend, but I ate it.
I also realized ... it was a dream!
That was the story of my purple, radioactive, perilous, petrifying pizza
with pickles, and pepperoni, and plums, and pears, and pies, and pineapples.

Locust Lake
by Pratham Soneja

When I emerge
From the cottage
The sun shines on my face
I look over the lake
And I see the
Glory of Locust Lake

Bumblebee
by Madilyn Lavin

Bumblebee, bumblebee,
Flying home
Bumblebee, bumblebee,
To the honeycomb.
Bumblebee, bumblebee,
In the sky
Bumblebee, bumblebee,
Flying by.
Bumblebee, bumblebee,
Getting home
Bumblebee, bumblebee,
In the honeycomb.
Bumblebee, bumblebee,
On the ground
Bumblebee, bumblebee,
Safe and sound.

Electrifying News About Electronics
by Shreya Rozario

Oh, where to start,
they're taking over the world part by part.
They steal your attention for hours and hours
It almost seems like they have powers!
And did I not mention the damage to your eyes,
oh boy, do I sound like your parents in disguise?
Each new morning brings a new creation,
Every version creates a new sensation!
The desire to keep up, though a source of inspiration,
To stay away would be a sure test of determination!
I sure am not denying,
The news about electronics is indeed electrifying!!
Though after all I've said, this might be ironic
But I too do use electronics.
There is probably more to say,
But for now I'll call it a day!

The School Year!
by Heidi Polakovsky

Suzie loved school, but one day a green ghoul frightened her
while she was eating from a bowl.
And she hasn't gone to school today.
And while she was homeschooled the same green ghoul frightened her
and she spilled some ink that made him pink.
And he ran away, he never frightened Suzie.
She went to school and ate from the same bowl, but there was no ghoul.

Ahh, Food
by Juliana Vasquez

The smell of fresh pie out of the oven,
The sound of butter sizzling,
The crunch of eating chips,
Ahh,
Isn't that delicious?
Freshly made glaze poured on top of donuts,
Oozing all the way down,
A nice warm bowl of hot soup in the cold weather,
Making hot chocolate with marshmallows,
Ahh,
The warm heat,
Or sitting next to a campfire making s'mores,
Yum!
Now you should know how delicious food is,
Cherish food!

Fall
by Alexandria Rosar

Fall is my favorite season
And I have more than one reason
I love the colors of the leaves on the trees
And the beauty of them blowing in the breeze
I love a bonfire at night
It creates such a beautiful sight
I love playing outside during the day
Jumping in leaves and sometimes the hay
A pumpkin patch trip can be a lot of fun
Especially when you find the perfect one
I think the fall is the best
But all good things must come to a rest
I am sad to see the fall come to a finish
As winter arrives the leaves diminish
I'll get through the snow, the spring, and the sun
And get back to the fall, my favorite one!

Puppies
by Nellina Guadagnoli

Chihuahua, pug, beagle, puppies, mutt, hound
Whiskers, big ears, small, big, white, tan, fast, slow
Colorful, tall, wet nose, wet tongues,
furry, wet, black, eat
Cute, fun, love, play, wag
Jumpy, cute tail, sheltie, small
Puppy, intelligent, big, bark, smart
Shih Tzu, excited, love, kind, awesome, great

The Beautiful Game
by Benjamin Norelli

You can feel movement
And skill in the player
When you step on the field
You can hear the crowd
Screaming your name
Like you've finished a magisterial goal
When you watch playmakers play the great game
Soccer inspires you
Step up to that extraordinary level
Pass
Shoot
Score!
Now YOU are the playmaker
Everything in soccer is magic
And players make that magic!

Halloween
by Tessa Vanasco

Candy, candy, oh so sweet!
Candy, candy, what a treat!
All the colors, oh so bright!
All the colors, what a delight!
All the flavors, what a treat.
All the flavors, all you can eat!
All the tastes. All the colors, oh so bright!
There's no need to fight! Only take one.
No need to knock. Oh! What fun!
Costumes as far as I can see!
Vampires, wolves, unicorns too.
Oh no, there's no more candy!
Oh no way, too scary!
Welp! We should call it a night!
Oh, trick-or-treating, what a delight!

Color
by Nate Plaksienko

Oh color;
Oh color.
You take us out of white and black.
Red.
Orange.
Yellow.
And green.
Rainbows, plants, animals;
And everything.

The Cat
by Lucia Dyson

There was once a cat named Jack,
He was really fat,
Jack did not want to attack,
So he sat,
In the bed he just bit,
To see the mouse,
He wanted to pounce,
Jack pounced the mouse,
But it ran away,
Clearly, it was not Jack's day,
Jack was a lazy cat,
He did not get on things stat,
When he caught a mouse,
Jack felt like he wanted to joust.

I Met a Pig
by Sabrina Kossup

I met a pig, it was pink
It was not big, it liked to blink
I named her Sunny, Sunny is so fun
She is very funny, she loves to run
I invited her parents to dinner
We played a game and Sunny was the winner
We all had a great time and our dinner was so fine
I asked my family if they can stay for the night
My family said alright
Sunny's family was so happy
Although they were all mappy
We all slept in our beds
Sunny slept with her doll named Zed
We all fell sound asleep
When it was morning they all took in their Jeep

Rainbow
by Yvonne Garner

Rainbow
The beautiful colors in the light
Rainbow
The colors shine just as bright.
Rainbow
It keeps me sad when it goes out in the night.
Rainbow
I like to see it when I fly my kite.
Rainbow
I want to see another rainbow at first sight.

October Chill
by Cristina DiPaolo

The green leaves are turning red, orange, yellow and brown
The chilly breeze is flowing into the town
Squirrels are snickering as they climb up the trees
When I realize it's October, I just feel, free
The wind is brushing back my hair
You know what they say, fall hair don't care
At nighttime, the jack-o-lanterns lighten their face
Kids, like me, running to different places
Screaming, "Trick or Treat!"
And others have candy so sweet to eat
The leaves crunch as I step on them
But I think jumping in them is more fun!
Now, who doesn't love October?
Absolutely no one!

It's the Little Things In Life
by Ronae Berresford

Forget about the times your heart filled with strife,
My dad used to say, "It's the little things in life."
Remember the times you've jumped up in joy,
Or donated a few or all of your toys.
Forgive and forget about all disagreements,
Instead be proud and focus on all your achievements.
The birds, the plants, the sky, and the bees,
The clouds, the dogs, the animals, and the trees.
These are things that bring me joy,
That and all my little toys.
"It's the little things in life," my dad used to say,
Remember these times and don't throw them away.
They make you happy and fill you with glee,
The little things do that for me.

Wilderness
by Timothy VanKleeck-Eagan, Jr.

Fluffy snow is falling from the sky
The ground is covered with white snowballs
The squirrels are in the trees
The leaves are falling off the trees
The snow is crunchy when I walk on it
The birds are moving south
I feel fluffy snow on the ground
The breeze is blowing
In the cave there is ice
Covering the ground is ice
The leaves start to grow back
Squirrels are gathering nuts
Acorns are dropping
Rain is falling

Pale Moonlight
by Cristopher Rodriguez

As the sun sets in the dark starry night,
a new beauty arrives, it's the Pale Moonlight.
On top of the lake a light shines with Passion and fright,
before your eyes, it's the Pale moonlight.
On a stormy night, when rain hits the top of your umbrella,
Its light will flow and make you go, "Whoa."
Now that the night is over and the Sun will show
that means the Pale moonlight has to go.
But maybe another night you will see the spectacular glow
of this beautiful sight, the wonderful Pale Moonlight.

The California Wildfire
by Vainavi Pandilwar

In the year of 2018,
Something happened like a bad dream.
The morning sky looked like night,
All the bodies were filled with fright.
From the sky fell the ash,
The firefighters were on the dash.
The morning sky was midnight dark,
It all looked like burned bark.
Ash fell in piles so deep,
People were trying not to weep.
The flames of the fire were up in a flare,
It all truly was a nightmare.
All the victims were under a scare,
That is because they were under the fire's glare.

Perfect Pizza Pie
by Grace Blasdell

I had a pizza,
It came to life,
I named it Paul,
He was my pet,
He could paint,
He liked purple,
He liked panthers,
He liked paper,
He was like a dog,
He was perfect,
He was a perfect pizza.

Mathematics Maniacs
by Julia Delgado

Math is fun! Isn't it for everyone?
Math is my favorite, at least.
Math is everywhere. In signs, in rhymes,
and even how many seeds are in limes.
Math includes multiplication, division, addition,
subtraction, fractions, and many more to learn, for a future job.
And in return, you use math to count money.
We start as seeds so tiny and small,
but don't give up and fall.
Just keep trying and you will be a pro.
You will just be counting and never say no to go to the show.
Math is all 'round.
Just look and see and you will be flying like a bee.

Turning Out
by Sabrina Lopez

Today I lie in bed thinking of what you said,
"You have turned out fine aren't you just divine."
As I think it over, I turn over letting the blood rush to my head.
Now I think harder, and I said: "I'm turning out fine?"
I know that's not right, I am only 10 and I have turned out then?
I start to think it over, about how I have turned out.
But nothing comes to my head.
I figured out that we are all unique.
And nonetheless, we should all agree.
In and out we're beautiful creatures
Weird no matter what.
We're different, we're the same
And that is the beauty of us.
So let's care for each other while we still have the trust.

Books
by Simone Crome

If you want to read a book
Open it up and take a look
Cause if you're staring at the cover
Then you won't discover
That the queen that you rely on
Actually had her eye on
Stealing the king's gold
So maybe now you will be bold
And read chapter one
But don't think you are done
After reading chapter one
There's lots more to come
The book has only just begun.

Outstanding Beauty
by Jada Branch

My grandmother is my sun.
Who brightens up my day one by one.
She's beautiful, kind, loving, and strong like a vine.
Her hugs are as sweet as honey,
They are so much better than any money.
When I grow I want to be just like her.
Such a sweet flower, with so much power.
She is my best friend.
My love for her will never end.
She is everyone's matron.
Such a magical person
Who always makes me be my best version

Laying On a Sidewalk
by Kellen McGoldrick

Laying on a sidewalk,
Its dull white petals,
Its bright green stem,
An unusual sight I see.
I walked right by it thinking, "Ugly,"
And she said, "Don't just walk by, feel some empathy."
Pushed to do something, I picked it up,
And laid it down with friends.
"Thank you," she smiled up at me,
I felt an emotional impact that day,
That changed my life forever!
That little white flower,
Laying with its friends.

Rainy Day
by Caylin Raymond

Looking out my window
Such a rainy day
Watching it fall down
Wish I could go outside and play
Laying in my bedroom
Hear the thunder roar
Looking out the window
Watch it rain some more
Late in the night
Watch the lightning strike
Laying in my bed
Bundle up tight

God
by Ashlynn Czebiniak

God is love.
God is joy.
God is joyful.
God died on the cross.
And rose again in three days.
After God arose He was on Earth for 40 days.
God went to Heaven.
And God sent the Holy Spirit.
The Holy Spirit came to the people.
The people fell on their knees.
The Holy Spirit blessed them,
And kept them safe.

Mom
by Cierra Nicotra

Mom,
I love you
you care for me and you share with me
your hair is long just like your life
you're strong like a bull and allergic to wool
we play, we sway all day and every day
you like to sing, I like to swing and vise versa
your touch is calming and means everything to me
I love you.
every touch you give makes me live
you are the best of the world, the greatest of girls
I love you to the moon and back
Love, Sunshine Cierra

Cody
by Hailey Vidal

Cute, fluffy and brown
He's loving, caring and cool
Cody is my dog

Penguins
by Alessia Dragonetti

Flip, flop across the ice
waddling to the ocean
Splash! In they go
hunting for their next meal
After, they go home
ready to do it again tomorrow

The Seagull
by Madelyn Vetri

High and low,
Swooping and stooping.
Flying and diving.
He pauses, then attacks his innocent prey.
He continues on toward the setting sun.

ELA Is the Best
by Alessandro Paradiso

Reading is the best.
Writing is even better.
Letters look amazing when you put them all together.
Grammar is important.
Vocab is essential.
Fit the words where they go to make them residential.
Reading is the key to knowledge.
Read something interesting in your cottage.
Make sure to meet the authors and pay homage.
Writing voices your opinion.
Every sentence is a brainstorming minion.
If it goes viral, you can make a million.
Grammar is key to revising.
The difficulty is easy! It's surprising!
Make sure to study your space sizing.
Vocab helps you understand the text.
It helps you read some words that are complex.
Some of the words can leave you perplexed.
They make you want to say, "thank u, next".

Wind
by Julz Hobbs

I hear the wind moaning,
As I walk outside,
Its voice hissing,
Go back inside.
I ignore it,
And keep on trudging,
Through the leaves,
That cover the bare ground.

A Wonderful Summer
by Aine Skelly

Summer is a wonderful time
You can stay up late and play
Or go to the park and ride
Or trampoline all day.
Sleepovers are fun
Talking and laughing all night
Going on vacation.
Sometimes I fly my kite.

My School Grissom
by Camille Johnson

My school Grissom, is the one place to be
My school Grissom, is the place that's best for me.
Sun or rain, we're always there
To see what we can learn and share!
Grissom Gators are what we are,
Grissom Gators are real stars!
So, come on in and join the fun,
I promise you there is no need to run!

Oh, How
by Matthew Lawrence

Oh, how beautiful the sky is on a summer night.
Oh, why do they pollute my beautiful sky.
They never think about those poor clouds up above.
Oh, how my heart is filled with sorrow.
When will those big companies know,
That the world matters, not just you.
Let's all strive to be better,
At saving the world from its destruction.

The Scared Mouse
by Blaine Harrison

The cat and the mouse ran around the house.
The house spit out the cat and the mouse into space.
Where they lived in a couch in space.
They floated in their couch.
But a louse lived in the couch
which kicked them out of the couch
back in the house where they lived happily ever after.

Summer
by Deanna Rotos

Summer is the season, to laugh, play and dash.
Jump in the pool and make a big splash!
Out for dinner with the fam, enjoy some dessert while you can.
Hang out with friends, ride bikes all day.
Go to the beach, and play some volleyball along the way.
Some time with cousins would be great!
Until next year we'll have to wait!

Dreaming
by Alexis McNall

The last thing you hear are crickets chirping
and the sound of your soft and slow breathing as you doze off.
The next thing you hear is nothing. Absolutely nothing.
Everything is black.
Soon, everything starts to fade into sight.
Your own house. From the outside.
How did I get out here? You think as you walk back into the house.
The next thing you see is your parents, sitting at the table,
with your siblings next to them. "Hi!" You say. They don't respond.
"Hello!" You say again, confused. What is going on?
You walk further into the house,
only to find that you can't get to the other rooms.
"Guys. It's not funny. Stop joking around."
They all turn their heads toward you,
revealing their ugly and distorted faces.
You feel a mixture of pure shock and fear as you run.
You can't make it out of that room. They walk closer.
You're cornered. They walk close, then closer, then ... "GASP"
You wake up in a cold sweat, shivering.
You look around. You are in your room.
Phew, you think as you realize that it was just a dream.
You start feeling sleepy again. You lay back down.
The last thing you hear are crickets chirping
and the sound of your soft and slow breathing as you doze off ...

Books
by Benjamin Anderson

Take a look,
it's in a book.
If you read some more,
you might get hooked.
Turn the page,
it's all the rage.
Make your eyes hover
over its beautiful cover.
When you get to the end,
it is your friend.
So take a look,
it's in a book.

Nature
by Ayse Arvas

I am nature, I am nature
God created me
I have different colors
Like green of a maple tree
I love blooming flowers
And growing new plants
I serve fruits and vegetables to human beings
I let animals drink from my bodies of water
I am happy to see everyone smile
I thank God for making me beautiful
I thank people who keep me clean
I hope everyone will always love me

Spring
by Michaela Hardy

I look around and see the green grass on the ground for miles
see the pink, green, blue, yellow, and purple of the flowers
See the red and green apples on the trees
see the pink and white buds on the leaves
look at the sky and see the white clouds floating by
see the pink, orange, yellow and blue
This is New York and I love it
I grew up with these things all around me,
my favorite part of the day,
the outdoors
the outdoors
the outdoors!

Pools
by Brianna Pagliuca

Pool
Let me soak my feet,
Have me feel the heat
Each one is better than the last
Just have a big old blast!

Ice Cream Sundaes
by Ariana Tzagarakis

Ice cream is really good
It's very tasty and there are many different flavors and toppings.
You can eat ice cream in a cone or a cup.
There are many different kinds of cones and cups.
Wow! Ice cream is really good!

When I Die
by Mary Kate Russo

Although I'll have left, I won't truly be gone
At least now I can't do anything wrong.
When you're alive you cannot know
If your troubles are truly friends or foes.
When I die, I cannot be sure
If I needed to live for more
When I die- if at a young age
I will still be with you, just beyond your gaze
And when death is near me-
And I know it's the end-
I'll sit down for some tea,
As if with a friend

Loving Yourself Is What Matters
by Emelia Feger

There are many different types of humans
Black, White,
Skinny, Fat,
Tall, Short,
Poor, Rich,
Gay, Straight,
You are you.
It doesn't matter what other people think.
It's what you think that's important.
You are beautiful in your own way.
We are all humans, different and unique.
Love yourself- that's what really matters.

Eagle
by William Kaiser

A place full of life
deep inside the forest's heart,
it is what I am, but not who I am
your intense vision allows you to see the bright foliage
the fight for life will always go on, or will it?

Windy Day
by Noah Moore

Windy snow goes stinging across my face
It feels like a hurricane blowing around me
Snowflakes go gleaming around my face
As I can climb the Adirondack Mountains
It rips like once or twice
and a blizzard comes sliding around me.

Blake the Bunny
by Savannah Geniton

Amazing, playful, white
cute blue eyes
really floppy ears
has little feet but cute feet
a little nose and a mouth that's small
but very, very soft
he's very, very awesome
happy, clumsy
he has a cotton tail that's really soft
has little feet that are clean
Guess who ...

Drawing
by Audrey Beiler

Oh, how I love to draw
The feel of the paintbrush in my hand
Draw a leaf, draw a fern,
Draw a drummer in a big band
Draw with a paintbrush,
Or a pencil or pen
Draw a forest so green and so lush,
Draw whatever you want
Paint or Draw, Draw or Paint,
Draw till you faint
You can be an artist, don't mind the age
Be an artist at 12, 6, or 17, even 4.

Words
by Harper Hara

Words are hard to explain.
They are a string of letters
sewn together by the nimble voice
of a needle and thread.
They explain the existence of the moon,
the stars and the sun.
Even the whole universe
can be explained by words.

Birds, Birds
by Harrison Gebeloff

Birds, birds sing me a song,
while you sit on my shoulder all day long
Birds, birds, let's walk to the park
so we can sing and dance until it turns dark
Birds, birds, it's time to go rest,
so I'll bring you back home to your little nest
Birds, birds, sweet dreams to you
and I'll see you again when the sky turns blue

Winter Days
by Sophie Comerford

It's cold outside.
The air is fresh and crisp.
Fresh like the forest air. Crisp like biting into an apple.
I see a red cardinal.
Good luck, I think.
Then, I look outside the windows, and all I see is white.
White like the school floors. White like a shining star.
I go outside and roll in the snow.
I jump and swim in the endless sea of snow.
Now, Mama is calling me to dinner.
I make my way back home.
Inside, I am filled with warmth.
Papa is serving mashed potatoes with broccoli and gravy.
Soon, before I know it, it is time for bed.
Mama and Papa come to tuck me in.
They tell me how Christmas break is soon.
How on Christmas we have a big feast, and family come.
I can't wait for Christmas.
But soon, almost too soon, my world goes dark,
And I drift off to sleep.

Wilderness
by Grady Shea

All is great with the glow
of oh so glimmering snow.
Birds chirping right and left.
Finding food makes me feel a theft.
Every step gives off a new sound.
At this point, you can't even see the ground.

Snow Days
by Joseph Pirozzi

I like snow because you can do so much with it
Snow forts, snowmen, snow houses!
Oh! And Angels, don't forget!
I also love school days off
And hot chocolate stands
Or making cookies for Santa
When the snow covers the lands

The Man On My Street
by Nicolette Solano

The rain dripping over his head
he's laying there without a bed
his hands and feet, numb and cold
praying and wishing he had a home.
I go over and ask if he's alright
he looks at me then let's out a sigh
I go to the store, I buy everything he needs,
like water, blankets and more
I go back to him and I say, "Take this"
He says, "No"
I say, "I insist"
His eyes start to tear up, he takes the bag
I start to think how no one has done this before
He sits there on the concrete floor
As I start to cry, I prepare to say goodbye
I walk away
Everyone should do this
if you do
Here's a big Thank You!

Dog
by Sarah Angelucci

I am very cute
I bark at squirrels, cars, and deer
I walk with leashes

Fall Feelings
by Lucia Virgil

Love jumping in leaves
Thanksgiving and Halloween
We eat pumpkin pie

Candy
by Monika Janczuk

Candy, candy.
What a wonderful treat.
It's something so, so delicious to eat.
From swirly little lollipops to fluffy cotton candy,
all of the candies are really quite dandy!
It is sweet or sour, bitter or tough,
candy is yummy no matter what!
From small, beady Whoppers to big Twix bars,
candy is everywhere, maybe even on Mars!
Candy really is a good treat,
but make sure that you brush your teeth after you eat!

Please Mister Governor
by Isabella Linares

The hail is falling down
Two weeks are not sufficient to complete my projects
To develop ease with my teachers
Please Mister Governor
I recommend you be a patriot
and represent all New York children
let us master what we love
I don't want to lack an education
It will be to my benefit if you agree
I am in dismay to utter my last remarks to you
Please Mister Governor
don't let the hail fall, may I please go to school

Halloween
by Kayla Sutowski

Trick-or-treat!
I love to dress up and play!
My birthday is here!

The Deer In the Forest
by Olivia Genus

Summer forest, patch of sun,
Pretty doe, white spots, light brown,
Chasing her friend, circle sprint,
Happy, excited, deep down.

Val the Puffer
by Brenden MacWilliams

Very playful
Always having fun
Loving

Tussles at the algae
Hangry sometimes
Entertaining

Puffer
Unites with other fish
Food
Feisty
Energetic
Resists hunger for others

Fall Can Bring You Happiness
by Eliza Cook

You wake up and think about
the tons of leaves you will have to rake
you go outside and get the rake
you are so cold and now you have a stuffy nose
you say to yourself, how many leaves are there
you hope that the day will warm up
you are so happy when you finish the job
the sun comes out
you go out and play with your mom and dad
you play pass with the football and you are full of happiness!!

Trick Or Treat
by Sara Dzaferovic

Trick or treat
all those treats come to
me on Halloween.

Dogs
by Valentina Buono

Dog types
Old dogs
Good dogs
Small dogs

Allergic To the Sun
by Nicholas Cirillo

I planned a trip to outer space and invited my friends to come,
'cause if I didn't it would really be a bum.
But when I got up there, I noticed that I was allergic to the sun.
I felt the breeze, it made me sneeze, I knew I shouldn't have come.

The Peaceful Room
by Keira Bryson

The peaceful room, that's where I'll be.
Not in my room, not up a tree.
The library is where I like to sit;
I think it is the perfect fit.
The librarians have done a good deed,
Helping us with what we need.
Everywhere that you will look;
You may see some wonderful books.
From fiction to mystery;
Poems to history.
All you have to do is look,
Some will even help you cook!
I truly think that you should come;
So many authors to decide from!
There are so many fun events,
You should attend, it just makes sense.
I truly think that you should go.
It's very exciting; believe me, I know.

Winter Comfort
by Justin Llego

Chicken noodle soup -
with extra hot sauce on top
and parmesan cheese

Why Can't I
by Antonia Brandt

I can do my homework
I can do my chores
But why can't I climb the trees?
Swim with the fish?
Why can't I climb up mountains?
Why can't I read all my books?
Why can't I?

Sleep
by Lillian Kovaleski

You need to get sleep without a peep.
You need to get sleep at night so your body is ready when a cold wants to fight.
You need to rest your brain so it does not need a cane.

Flip and Whiskers
by James McAuley V

Fussy about food
Loves fish
Inspiring
Playful

Always in trouble
Noticed always
Doing silly things a lot

Wants to be noticed
Helpful ... Not!
Idiotic sometimes
Super duper cats
Kid flip
Energetic
Rips open treat bags
Silly cat

2020 Rising Stars Collection

Soccer
by Olivia Mauceri

Soccer balls as round as a globe
Open fields as wide as space
Cleats as dirty as a robber's conscience
Coaches howling like the wind
Extra awesome goals made
Roaring crowds that sometimes fade

Halloween In Levittown 1985
by Joseph Skelly

On Halloween night
Kids dying of fright.
And teenagers driving in cars,
By them you were hit by candy bars.
There were people with eggs,
Chucking them at your legs.
Streets were covered in shaving cream,
And for this reason, the kids would all scream.
Mom trashed candy that was unwrapped,
After we feasted, we gladly napped.
Trick or treating was a fun time
But I can no longer think of a rhyme.

The Door
by Alyssa Nichter

A slight turn of a knob
A small push of a hand
A quick creak of a door
You open it and ...
What is behind it?
Do you know?
What things are inside it?
I wondered and so ...
I thought about what it could be
A person, a place, a thing?
Let's see!
I opened the door
And what did I see?
I took a small peek
And I saw me!
A mirror in a room
Behind a small door
I was quite disappointed
For I've seen me before

Flowers
by Valentina Lechner

Flowers are so beautiful.
Lilies are the best flowers.
On flowers there are seeds.
Water makes flowers survive.
Every flower is a different color.
Red is a color of a flower.
Some flowers smell good.

Davy Crockett
by Parker Cook

Davy was a father
A very good hunter he was
Valiant efforts were given to win elections
Yet through the madness of war he survived

Congress he was a part of
Rambling he did a lot of
On top of most things he was
Coonskin hats he was famous for wearing
Killing 105 bears in one season he has claimed
Eating freshly killed meat was one of his childhood favorites
Telling jokes was his specialty
Typically he told stories

My Ferret Marcus
by Blake Hatfield

Marcus the Mugger
Young

Furry and fat
Excitable
Rambunctious
Reckless
Enthusiastic
Tame

Meddler
Active
Rowdy
Cute
Uncontrollable
Soft and squishy

Fall
by Joey Smith

The Cold wind Blows,
The hot wind slow.
Leaves Fall to the ground,
Making colors All around.

Oh, The Problems
by Mia Whyte

My leg had an itch.
My eyes started to twitch.
Then, my computer screen glitched,
Oh, the problems.
My cat was on a mat.
While chasing a rat.
Hitting the rat with a bat,
Oh, the problems!

Stepping Into Fall
by Brodie Murray

Trees get ready for winter, like snakes shedding skin.
Red, orange and brown piles line the path, waiting for the cold snap to being.
Dogs fetch fallen branches and chase the stray leaves,
Kids run around in the park in a cool autumn breeze.
Warm apple cider makes after school fun,
Gingerbread house making season has definitely begun!
Jackets are brought out of the closet, pant lengths get longer,
Squirrels bury plenty of nuts to help make them stronger.
Bears, bats and snails snuggle down for a few months to sleep,
Not all animals have warm coats like alpacas and sheep!
Sunset arrives early and sunrise appears late,
Turkeys pace anxiously, it's close to "that" date!
Fireplaces light up to help warm hands and toes,
There's nothing like feeling that first snowflake land on your nose.
The sun may still be shining but it's all very clear,
Summer has left us and Fall is now here!

Winter
by Archer Engels

A soft white blanket of snow
covers the moonlit hills,
frosting on a cake.
Flowers of all colors
poke out from the dunes,
colorful gems.
A hound bays at the moon
as a watchful owl slices
through the sky like a knife.
A wolf as quiet as a mouse
sniffs the cold air,
it stalks its prey.
An elegant stag walks
proudly through the woods.
The trees converse
while snowflakes of all shapes
gracefully float down
from the starry sky.

DIVISION II

GRADES 6-8

Run Turkey
by Merrit Cauchi

Run turkey run.
The farmer's got a gun
The wife has the oven hot
So run and run
So you don't get served between a bun.

No One Is Perfect
by Sarah Merlo

The earth can be what it wants to be.
But you can be who you want to be.
Flowers bloom and so do we.
Our love is like no other love.
But you can be loved by whoever it may be.
The earth blooms as we change who to be.
Waves crash and so do we.
No one is perfect.
But you can be who you want to be.

Be You!
by Andrea Storvig-Newson

Who cares if you are different from the rest,
you are unique and do your best.
All you have to be, is true to yourself and kind,
there will always be happiness for you to find.
In every challenge you're a champion,
no need to worry, you've already won.
You can be brave, smart and bold,
you can shine bright like a piece of gold.
Be confident and never shatter,
because everything you do will always MATTER.

Jelly Journeys
by Agnieszka Nalepa

I am a jellyfish, I swim in the sea
I will sting if you get close to me
When I sting it hurts for hours on end
I'm sorry I had to my little friend
But it is my instinct to do such things
I know it really, really stings
If you don't know, I am a jellyfish called "The Man of War"
It looks like I have a purple core
You can find me in tropical places
Whenever people see me I see scared faces

Ocean
by Trista Somerville

The ocean is calm
The fish follow the waves
Bigger and bigger the waves get
A storm is coming
Big, heavy dark clouds come rolling in
A rainbow goes over the ocean
A dolphin jumps out of the water
The ocean is calm again.

Rusting Away
by Michael DeChiaro

Bewildered souls lose their way
Bums of the world don't see the day
Busy people don't get to play
Retired workers just get to stay
Train conductors stay on the tracks
Personal trainers never slack
Businessmen stab each other in the back
People rust away into nothing but black

Fall
by Olivia Carr

In the fall you will start to see
All the colors that cover the trees
Bright red, orange, and yellow leaves
As the wind begins to blow
The birds begin to get into their flow
Beginning the travel south in their flocks slow
The trees will start to turn bare
The cold chill will enter into the air
And a long nap begins for the bear

Art
by Natalia Piekarski

The stroke of a brush on a canvas.
The rainbow that emerges when a colored pencil draws.
The bruised hands that sculpt.
The brush dripping with colors.
The glee it brings to a child when they let a crayon work its magic.
The felicity a soul finds in the illustration of art.
The lullaby that plays in the mind when the pencil hits paper.
A rainbow of colors.
A rainbow of colors is just what art was made to be.

With a Book
by Rachel Rappoport

In a different world
Oblivious
Word after word pulls me in
Drawn to the world of a book
On the edge of my seat
Leaning in
I feel like I'm there
Not here
Not the couch
Not my house
Wonderland
Poem rhythm rhyme
I'm lost to the time
An hour may pass
And me you will find
On my bed with a book
On a couch with a book
In my room with a book
With a book

The Dark Place
by Delia John

Sometimes late at night, I drift into the dark place,
where the birds are calling and the trees are falling
and everything is upside down.
Wind blows through the ceiling and the walls behind me are all peeling
and everything is dark in the dark, dark place.
But suddenly my hand falls on some kind of switch,
what horrors lie at the flip of this switch?
What creatures and monsters will suddenly appear,
when I flip this switch standing right here?
What insects and bugs will crawl up my spine,
while my hand touches its center line?
Will the walls collapse right on top of me,
or will I drown in piping hot tea?
Because you never know what is hard to see,
when the dark place stares down on me.
Will the shiny black leaves blow me into a tree,
while the night owl feeds me to its babies?
An eye for an eye, an ear for an ear, but what future seeks for me to hear?
What diamonds and gems will shine so divine,
only to find it was all just a lie.
So what will this switch do, just wait and see,
it could send monsters and insects and fright-
Oh, look at that!
It turns on the lights

Basketball
by Tyler Cook

A shot of a man down, a ball flying
Team yelling and ref whispering, man crying
Fly high, don't touch a thing
It goes in, we win
Cheer and laughter fill the noise
No one knows how to feel great
We won, it feels so fake
It can't be true
A man said no matter what
You win in your heart
I won and my heart exploded
On the ground
No one around
All by myself
I will treasure this memory for the rest of my life
Teammate helps me up
I get home, I eat a treat
We won, it was because of me
Follow your dreams, anything can happen
As you see it can
Anything can be true if you believe

Where I'm From
by Travis Adamczyk

I am from my mom, my dad,
my soccer-playing brother and my baton-twirling sister.
I am from my awesome dog, Kona.
From cheerful Christmas with caring family.
I am from going to my great-grandmother's house for Christmas Eve every year.
I am from going to my grandma's house for buttery toast.
From sneaky hide-and-seek with my siblings and cousins.
I am from going to stunning car shows with Grandpa.
I am from jumping on a small trampoline with my brother and sister.
From the boom of me and my siblings falling with our roller skates
I am from slipping while ice skating with my siblings.
From going to amazing AMC with my dad and siblings.
I am from watching an every week movie at my house.
I am from going shopping at ShopRite with my dad.
From going to giant Great Adventure.
I am from working hard and being patient.
From seeing marvelous movies and eating crunchy popcorn with my uncle.
From eating prized pizza and chicken tenders.
I am from hanging out with my funny friends.
I am from playing scoring soccer.
From going to fabulous Florida.
I am Travis Adamczyk

The Wisdom Within Me
by Serena Carnahan

I remember thinking, when I was small,
How will I look when I grow tall?
I had the future on my mind,
While visions of a new me slowly aligned.
I was very curious, you must see,
To know what great things I could be.
I imagined myself with every good trait,
For I knew it was I who determined my fate.
Will my hair be cut short, or will it grow long?
Will I make good decisions, or do everything wrong?
But I soon figured out that I shouldn't worry,
Considering when you think about it, what's the hurry?
So I came to the conclusion that I should just be,
Because if you want to be successful, that's the key.
And now that I am older, I know that I was right,
To think that if you be yourself, you'll make it through the plight.

The Sun's Riddle
by Iman Umar

The story they told was different from the rest
It was about buildings, how different could it get
But it was absolutely, without hesitation, the best
It was peculiar in many ways, because that's how the buildings and the sun met
The sun rose up each day
The buildings were up looking above at the sun
questioning how high the sun really was
The buildings wanted to get as tall as the sun. There had to be a way
The buildings talked, searched for a way
but they couldn't find one, probably 'cause there really wasn't one.
But the sun enjoyed herself and played along.
She told the buildings all they needed to do was move
Now a building couldn't do that. The buildings told the sun that she was wrong
The sun said, "Did you ever try to move? I really do disapprove."
One building tried to talk to the sun
and tell her that they have tried but it doesn't work
Well the sun took a deep breath and told them there was no way to get taller
The buildings were shocked and told the sun that she was a jerk
The sun laughed but asked the buildings why they didn't like being smaller
The buildings said that they felt weak and powerless
Well the sun looked sympathetically and told the buildings they were not weak
and they were not powerless and that they were just buildings
And yes the bigger buildings are intimidating and scary
but they were perfect other than being colorless
The buildings saw the lesson of being true to themselves,
after that the sun and the buildings became best friends,
and they were always chilling

Pets
by Calum Mcalister

Pets are much more than animals.
They are part of me.
Whether it's fish, cats, dogs, or even snakes.
Which pet you own is a choice you make.
I own some fish and also a cat.
Some animals are skinny, some are fat.
All pets are different, just like you or me.
Some pets are cool, while some are scary.
They can range in color, from navy blue to cherry.
Pets make strange noises like glub, glub or meow.
Some pets are mean and their bite makes you say ow.
I have owned pets since I was born.
When they die, it makes your heart feel torn.
Most animals are wholesome creatures,
Everyone likes them, from soldiers to teachers.
Animals have been with me for all of my life.
They have made a bond with me stronger than a knife.

Where I'm From
by Estefania Banos

I am from being the girl who always listens
Being the sweet girl that includes everyone.
And having my grades above 87,
I am from my mom, a nail artist.
My dad, the manager of a car wash.
From my brother, Christian, who plays 3 sports.
To my sister, Vanessa, who's a professional photographer.
My other sister, Leslie, who's a spectacular dentist for kids.
I am from my dad's delicious juicy homemade hamburgers.
To Rita's savory watermelon chip ice cream with twist custard.
My mom's tasty homemade pasta.
I am from reading a scary or mystery book on Friday nights.
From hanging out with my friends at Air Trampoline or the park.
To succeeding in playing the piano and the saxophone.
I am from playing soccer on Saturday mornings.
To always being a fast runner.
From playing football on a bright sunny day with my brother.
I am from the quotes, "Always try your best."
"If you want something, earn it."
To keeping my word or my promise, no matter what.
To being the youngest sibling.
I am Estefania Banos

Knock Down the Wall
by Maizie Baunoch

There is a wall
A wall that sucks us in
We must knock down this wall
For everyone to win.
It's the wall of Afghanistan,
The wall of reflection.
Hidden from the world
The effect of election
It's the wall of shootings
The wall of suicide
The wall of troubled hearts
and twisted minds.
Knock down the wall!
Make peaceful fights!
Earn peace and trust, and equal rights!
For past this wall is a thing worthwhile
a patch of peace, like a distant isle
we must work together, hand and hand
To make our way to peace-filled land!

This Was What Happened
by Alice Rosenberg

The pavement folding into street
the tulips we planted last spring
the steady rhythm of my suitcase on concrete
This is what happened the morning of.
The gazebo benches outside our building
the wood was old and the green paint was peeling
the ringing phone vibrating off the trees
This is what happened before the call.
The overly friendly driver, the East River to our right
the giant dog and taxi cab around the corner
This is what was on our way there.
The glass doors, the bronze arcs
the marble ramp leading down and down
This was his resting place.
The tan of his face, the pink of his shirt, the suitcase in his hands
This was the last time I saw him. Alive.
Swollen arms, swollen feet, swollen bags full of liquid food.
This was really the last time I saw him.
The books basking in sunlight,
the wall of pictures, the sun's single shining ray
This was his real resting place.
The doctors' nod, the line slowing from
mountains to valleys to hills to bumps to a line.
This was when he died.

Where I'm From
by Mario Aquilone

I am from the stiff turf of a soccer field,
from going to Saturday soccer games.
I am from flag football on Friday,
I am from Sunday night basketball with friends.
I am from trips with my soccer team to Hershey,
from going to Florida with Papa and Mum-Mum.
I am from having a hectic vacation with my family,
to even crazier ones with uncles and aunts.
I am from Romeo's pizza on Fridays,
to my Dad's top-secret chili recipe.
I am from bountiful breakfasts on Easter mornings,
to huge cookouts at my beach club.
I am from Bella, my twin sister,
to Nicco, my older brother in middle school.
I am from Dad, who works in the city,
to Mom, who works from home.
I am from being the youngest in the family,
from nutty sleepovers.
I am from joking with friends.
I'm Mario Aquilone

I've Gone Mad
by Kira Heckman

The Mad Hatter, was a bad actor.
He showed the world he'd gone mad.
He didn't believe it, but he knew it.
Going mad ain't that bad.
He convinced a girl, that she should be glad she was mad.
When she went home they put her in a mad house.
They said, "She's lost her mind!"
but she said, "I haven't lost it, he's got it."
And the Hatter knew he's now got it.
He had a mind, her mind and he stole it.
But he didn't want to return it.
He was tired of being called crazy.
He knew they were all dazy.
Dazy still doesn't mean he's not crazy.
Crazy ain't bad, but he was still hazy.
His life flourished, much like a daisy.
Alice broke out and went even more lazy.
Left tracks to the death of Gracie.
Alice fed Gracie a spoonful of Tabun.
Hatter knew she'd done it, but Alice also demolished him.
Now Alice is the only mad one.
- Inspired by "Alice In Wonderland" by Lewis Carroll

Dark Place
by Hannah Mikovich

It is dark,
So chilling,
Yet so moist.
The air is pungent and moldy.
Full of amorphous shadows.
Filled with faint noises.
The stairs are creaky.
A hallway of darkness,
Of figures,
Of fears.
A heartbeat loudly roars from my chest.
Is it the Boogie Man?
The Grim Reaper?
Better run,
Better sprint in terror!
Sprint to safety from this "Irrational Fear".
How silly of me, a lady of 14,
To be horrified of such a place,
Basement.

America the Beautiful
by Krishav Singla

The beautiful land that many call home
Has been ripped apart to the bone
People fight over the most foolish of things
Including but not limited to, race, colors and even wedding rings
Instead of standing together we are divided; we fall
We step on another's feet like we believe it's protocol
I will never and can never understand
How can you turn your back,
On a country meant to be the dreamland?
We are unworthy of the privileges, with them we attack
As few join together and lead, many fall back
A country filled with violence and dread
America is being ripped to shreds
Instead of going to fight
Join together and become the light
There is enough darkness in the world
So why bring the dark to America so it can unfurl?
United we stand
Divided we fall
So let us unite and join hands!
We mustn't bawl.
To become the land
To become the land that I live in
To becoming America the Beautiful!

Dear Dreamer
by Angelina Martinez

Dear Dreamer,
It's been a long time, dearie.
You haven't written in a while.
Is it because your eyes have grown bleary?
We've forgotten your writing style.
We miss you, doll.
Only you would know.
Have your tales grown tall?
Or does your knowledge need to grow?
It's changed, your demeanor.
The colors are no longer stark and contrast.
The trees no longer grow greener.
The spell cannot be recast
You once loved our world.
But now it turns gray.
The pages are no longer unfurled.
There is not much else to say.
Do not forget us, you must.
Your ways have turned bland.
But gold doesn't turn to rust.
Do you understand?
Always and Forever, your Imagination

Where I'm From
by Hannah Jefferson

I am from my happy hygienist working Mom,
and my intelligent IFF working Dad.
I am from my amazing working aunts,
To my funny uncles.
I am from my glamourous grandparents.
I am from my baseball batting brother,
and shooting basketballs with my brother.
From Sunday Fundays with family.
I am from crazy Christmas family gatherings.
I am from amazing Atlantic City trips,
from family trips to Mexico.
I am from goofing around with Gabby,
to swimming in cold pools with friends.
From scooter Saturdays with my friends.
I am from beautiful beach mornings,
to swimming with slimy feeling dolphins.
I am from flipping around at gymnastics.
I am from Mom's fried pork chop Fridays
to taco Tuesdays in Mexico.
I am from Thanksgiving dinner and Grandma's house.
I am Hannah Jefferson.

People Are People
by Sarah Riether

Go put on your jersey,
Play your football game.
Don't wear makeup,
Don't be weak.
Be the person you're expected to be.
Go put on your dress,
Put your makeup on.
Don't play sports,
Don't be strong.
Let the men do it for you.
But,
Girls can play sports
And be strong.
Boys can wear makeup
And bake.
People want to be
Themselves
And if you don't like that,
whatever.

The Importance of Tolerance
by Anupama Iyer

It is important that everybody is treated fairly
With kindness and respect
No matter what they believe
Everyone should treat others the way that they want to be treated
While diversity is the spice of life
It can cause some people to feel some hatred
While for some, it causes joy
For others, it causes a quarrel
A world without diversity is like an artist's pallet without color
It is sad that people do not treat others fairly due to disabilities,
religion, race, and other differences
The world would be a better place if people learned to accept
the ideas and beliefs of others
Awareness and understanding leads to tolerance
The world should spend less on bombing and war, and more on education
Sometimes, people do not realize the battles that others are fighting
As we learn to embrace each other in spite of our preferences
People should not act like the jury and adjudicator
No matter who people are, they should walk with their heads held high
And they should never feel self-conscious if they have disabilities
What everyone needs is love, empathy, and acceptance
Putting differences aside will make the world a better place

You
by Nicole Hollinger

It takes guts to dream big dreams.
It takes a specialty to be who you are.
It takes guts to see big things.
To learn, to grow,
Knowing what you know.
It takes guts to move forward in the direction
of all your dreams that need to be accomplished.
Without guts, you would never reach the stars.
Because, you are an excellent, special, wonderful star
in a universe of planets and suns.
When you can't see the finish line,
Or when your dreams seem hard to find,
Know that your heart will lead you there one day.
In all that you do,
And all that you say,
You are a million times AWESOME every day!
So, be happy, bold, intelligent, energetic,
thoughtful, colorful, creative. In other words,
BE YOU!

Where I'm From
by Gabriella Gonzalez

I'm from the crack of a softball till sunset,
From Yankees with Pa,
I'm from Manhunt till midnight,
From Facetiming cousins.
I'm from Wiffle ball with neighbors,
From playing tug-of-war with Apollo,
I'm from going to Sandy Hook,
From hearing crashing crystal clear waves.
I'm from going to QuickChek,
from hanging out with friends,
I'm from Starbucks for food and drinks,
From going for ice cream with Alexandria.
I'm from a brainy mother,
From a stockbroker father
I'm from an enjoyable sister,
From an athletic brother.
I'm from hanging with Hannah,
From going in the pool,
I'm from getting ice cream
From watching Netflix.
I'm Gabby Gonzalez

Tuckerman
by Jessica Russo

Tuckerman
My favorite dog
My best friend
The one and only

Snow
by Emily Angelo

White glitter covers the ground.
It sparkles in the moonlight.
When you look out the window,
you can see a beautiful winter wonderland.
Snowflakes everywhere you go!
Although snow may be a beautiful sight,
it can be tragic.
Thick ice on the road.
Snow pilling up on sidewalks.
Ice sticking on your car.
Slippery sidewalks.
The dead of winter.
The most beautiful sights seem to distract us from
the bad sides of things.
Like snow.
Snow sparkles in the moonlight.
Oh what a beautiful sight.

Opinions Don't Always Matter
by Jamie Calabrese

Social media, a thing we love.
Social media, a thing we abuse.
Opinions, likes, dislikes
Comments, a voice we never heard
We are like puppets on strings,
going along with what they say.
Take a moment.
Realize how lucky you are,
How special you are,
You are a fish in a sea
With 7 billion others
But guess what? You're the only one
With that unique face of yours.
As Joel Osteen says, "People have their right to their opinion
and you have the right to ignore it."
So overall people say things but I don't have to listen
That's my right

Rue
by Austin Fox

Oh Rue, Oh Rue
Everybody loved you
Sad you had to go so soon
Just know we still love you

Darkness
by Kylie Miller

The darkness greets me
In the night sky.
The air so cold
As it enters my lungs.
Not able to see
What is in front of me.
I take a step forward.
Not knowing where to turn next.
Feeling so hopeless and unsure,
I need to make the right decision.
I take a step forward.
Moving forward,
Improving on my past mistakes.
Learning and growing,
Making the right choices.
Finally,
The sun has risen.

Where I'm From
by Giuseppe Virgilio

I'm from winning shiny hockey medals,
To playing other sports.
I'm from going to a hockey stadium,
To chowing down on Chinese food.
I'm from eating ice cream,
To my aunt's dogs, Killian, the Cane Corso, and Dublin, the American bulldog.
I'm from my family.
To playing with my playful baby cousin, Peyton,
I'm from fly-fishing on my uncle's brother's big boat.
To playing with friends in my neighborhood,
I'm from all types of animals in the wild.
To graphic novels,
I'm from traveling to Washington, D.C., Boston, Massachusetts.
To Mrs. Szotack and our crazy class pet rat
I'm from eating candy corn,
To counting my money.
I am Giuseppe Virgilio!

Art
by John Paolillo

Art is like a wave
It makes me very happy
Art warms my kind heart

Winter
by Michael Robert

I'd love to go out,
And play in the winter snow,
But my bed trapped me

My Dog
by Jocelyn Robinson

I watch my Dog
Run side to side trying to catch leaves
She was as black as a jacket
With a white chest
She was finally able to catch one leaf
Then she lay down to take a break

Where I'm From
by Khloe Martori

I am from the thigh throbbing football games.
I am from dawn to dusk soccer practices.
From volleyball on the silky sand.
I am from dancing outside with friends.
I am from Mom's cheese-in-the-bacon-burger.
I am from Sunday ice cream delight.
From D'Amore dinners.
I am from jaw dropping JakeaBob's chicken wraps.
I am from Target runs for school.
From Kohl's Tuesday deals.
I am from cute Justice shirts.
I am a laugh with Mom, generous person.
I am from Mom, a hairdresser.
From Dad, a bus inspector.
I am from my intelligent little brother.
From my grumpy gaming brother.
I am from funny sleepovers,
To unbearable scary movies on Saturday.
I am from tag inside until Mom says no.
I am from my Ohio family reunions.
I am Khloe Martori.

God
by Isaac Ebright

God has lightning in his eyes
On His throne, He has the power
When we pray, He hears our cries
God can hear us every hour.

Family
by Will Parker

Can I have some help?
You ask your family
Even if you don't admit it
Maybe they help you a little bit
They'll help you with anything
All you have to do is give them a ring

Jelly Bean
by Olivia Hulse

My bunny is soft and loves to play
He has lots of toys that keep him at bay
With a bam and a boom, he keeps me up at night
But I always make sure he's alright
Jelly Bean, my rabbit, smells like hay
I'm so glad he's my rabbit, hurray!

Charlie
by Cory Stone

Charlie is a good boy.
He is very sweet.
Charlie is a good boy.
He is very neat.
Charlie is a good boy.
He is very brown.
Charlie is a good boy.
He will turn your frown upside down.
Charlie is a good boy.
He is a great dog.
Charlie is a good boy.
He loves to take a jog.
Charlie is a good boy.
He is very kind.
Charlie is a great boy.
He is all mine.
I LOVE CHARLIE!

The Stream
by Piper Snyder

Hear the trickle, that's the stream,
Heading toward its winter gleam.
I heard a popping sound at night,
Then, I was filled with fright,
and I saw the forbidden gleam,
as I ran from the stream.

A Day In the Snow
by Graydon Brugger

Bundle up
Get a shovel
Open the door slowly
Observe the magnificent snow.
Put my boot outside on top of the snow
Press down with my boot and hear a crunch
Shovel the fluffy snow off the sidewalk
Push the snow into enormous piles.
Go get a red sled
Fly down the hill
Construct jumps to fly off of
Contest who can get more air.
Go inside
Feel the warm heat
Drink hot chocolate
Take a nap

Water
by Gregory Boam

Water flows just like air,
But water cannot be found everywhere.
Healthy water is clean and pure,
Murky, muddy water is not what one looks for.
Pond water sits there still,
While the waterfall is like a big spill.
The water in the pond still lies in a hush,
The waterfall sounds like a rush.
It's a long walk to water,
One has a lot of time to ponder.
After all that time to think,
One deserves a little drink.
The long journey was hard and tough,
One hopes the water collected will be enough.
To see one's family's thirst quenched, fills one's heart,
One must go get more, now is a good time to start.

Winter Woods
by Katherine Craig

The trees breathe, swaying
Leaves descending over snow
The river runs cold

Beach
by Lena Walz

Wind was blowing in the air,
Sand oozes between my toes
Like water seeping into the ground,
Waves rapidly crash on the shore
Lying under an umbrella
Sun shining down on me
Commotion all around
Pelicans stealing food left and right
Dip my feet in the crystal-clear water,
The chilling water made me shiver,
Decided to build a sandcastle
Finished it with great joy
The waves then crashed
My castle went down
The day at the beach was a blast
Depressed to see it go by in a flash.

Importance of a Tree
by Emma Conklin

Trees.
Full of life and vibrant colors
But no one understands how much humans abuse the use of trees,
Once they are gone, there is no reverting.
Imagine a world with no trees.
Not so hard.
But in reality,
No trees equals the fate of mankind
Not every person takes care of the world gingerly,
We are maiming the one planet suitable for life,
With every tree cut causes pollution.
Global warming.
All I can do is write,
Write about the destruction we cause,
So the next time you see a tree,
Thank that very tree.

The Things We Do Not Notice
by Aaisha Khan

The things we do not care to notice,
such as a little flickered spark,
rule up into disasters,
scarring trees with a burnt "mark".
Oh the things we do not care to notice,
or, rather, the things we choose to ignore,
includes overpopulation,
and global warming's "lore".
Woe to mankind!
Me, myself, and I
only MY unfathomable pain.
Yet those who choose to die,
oh their deaths are in vain.
Go tuck your selfishness away!!
Go make somebody's day!
And then maybe such a world
will not be full of pain.

Where I'm From
by Sienna Strobel

I am from Chick-fil-A after hard work at cheer.
From meatloaf Monday and taco Tuesday.
I am from Dunkin' before school
I am from clear crystal waves.
From first surf competitions.
From morning and night surfing with my friend, Jillian.
I am from stunning winter snowboarding in the white snow.
I am from Puerto Rico every winter break for surfing.
From Dominican Republic every summer.
To summers in Argentina with old friends.
I am from holidays with my big loud Brooklyn family.
I am from Christmas treasure hunt to see who opens their present first.
To big meals on holidays.
I am from outgoing surfing dog.
To wacky cats that like to take showers.
I am from sleeping with my snoring dog.
From giving my dog a piece of dinner every night.
From the Bahamas and cooking with Kearstin.
I'm from a very fierce and positive family.
I'm from being healthy and athletic.
I am Sierra Strobel

I Hate You
by Scarlett Orluk

Love, the opposite of what I see when I look at you.
Love is kind, love is sweet, love is never-ending.
Love is a gift that you receive,
and you never know when it's coming.
Love is something that two people or things feel for each other,
but I do not feel that love for you.
For you I feel hate beyond compare, for you I feel sadness.
Love should be something that all experience and all get to cherish,
I know that you think that my love is with you,
but with you it is not and won't be for eternity.
I love bright and light things that make people smile,
not dark and depressing things that make you want to hide.
You make me feel dark and make me want to hide.
You make me feel sad and like darkness
and death are right around the corner.
I do not love you, I deeply despise you,
I hate you dear mosquitoes that bite my sides and make me want to hide.
I hate you mosquitoes and all that you do.

Hardworking Women In America
by Morgon Washington-Patterson

She wanted a full cup of smooth, clean water.
She wasn't headed to a sip of water from human needs.
She dreams for the weight of the enfeeble work to be knocked off her back.
Every day she carries large buckets of dirty water,
hands trembling, shoulders slouching, legs burning.
As it was the only thing she and her family could drink to survive.
She wished one day,
That the Sun will not beat down on her skin, as she feels like a burning paper,
getting lesser and weaker as the fire keeps spreading.
But symbolize as a beacon of hope towards the next puzzle pieces of her life.
As she is just the tiniest speck of dust to this ball of white, green, and blue.
But, she will try ...
No!
She will take strides toward
She has gone too far in life to collapse like a Jenga tower.
And will not stop going forward
Until answers to her questions start seeping into her body like a magnet.

Hope
by Greenleebay Baker

Why do we close our eyes when we cry,
when we pray, and when we dream.
It's because life is like a sunset, not everything is seen,
but it's felt deep in the heart.

Apex Dubs
by James Jordan

I love those Apex dubs
They make me want to give 1000 hugs.
When I get those Apex Dubs
I love Battle Royales, they make me say WOW!
I love surviving
I would love to get some Grub-Hub
and get a belly rub.
They are so nice, just like Christ
When I see, "You are the CHAMPION"
My eyes light up like the 4th of July!
Apex wins, when I win
I want to play a mandolin.
But when I lose
I would love to kick everyone
In the shin
My favorite is my Apex rank
That is so dank

Proud To Be Black
by Janiyah Johnson

Come back from Oakland, Mother said.
I'm black, I said, I'm proud to be
Some of y'all white folk don't know
the true me because of my skin tone
Cops think they can tell me what to do
they be like
drop it
lay down
hands behind your back
You have to ...
but really all I have to do is
be black and die.
It's funny how death is in a cop's gun
"If you see something, say something"
Well, I told the cops I almost got shot
They just look at my skin color
and act like they forgot

Seagulls
by Zach Snyder

Seagulls
On the sandy beach
Are so big and are mean
Stealing food on that giant seashore
Go away

Simple Colors
by Massimo Buonagurio

This poem is simple
You read that right
So let's talk about colors
From dark to light
Roses are red
Violets are violet
But some think they're blue
It may start a riot
Bananas are yellow
And so are pencils
But while eating bananas,
Do not use utensils
This poem is simple
So now you know
We talked about colors,
The colors of the rainbow

The Late Day
by Luke Whalen

As I walked through the door
Of my first period class
I reached in my pocket
For my hall pass
All the students looked at me
As if I was the star of a show
The teacher just kept writing
She didn't even know
I walked up behind her and said, "Ahem!"
To get her to turn around
But all she did was take my pass
And told me to go sit down
I walked to my seat, my face all red
As if it was burned by the sun
"I'll never do that again!" I said to myself
Being late is never fun

Dreamless
by Margaret Martinez

These dreams that haunt me in my sleep,
I lie awake and hope for peace.
But every night is always like,
these dreams I have in my sleep.
I one day wish that this will cease.
That I will get a dreamless sleep.

A Colorful Kingdom
by Anna Maliakal

A forest in fall
Always seems to call
For me to come
Into a colorful kingdom
Red, orange, and yellow leaves
Stole the green like thieves
But their bright color
Makes up for losing the summer
During this season
There is a reason
For animals to collect food
And find a place of solitude
The beauty of this time
Is truly divine
And a forest is where you can find
Fall defined

A Plea For Trees
by Esme McLaughlin

I have a bonsai in my room
It shuts out the darkness and the gloom
The tree may be small, but it helps me to breathe
It makes a big difference with every leaf
Outside my home, there are some oaks
I draw them sometimes, with pencil strokes.
Those trees are growing, and they're now so tall
But in some cases they're cut down for a store or a mall
The wood is used for several things
Papers and pencils and thrones for kings
In this world we should save the trees
They lessen air pollution and complement a breeze
I adore nature and you should too
Or we would not have oxygen and all turn blue
The animals and the children need a place to roam
So please protect the trees, our habitat and home.

The Hyena
by Logan Blackwell

Quick. Cackling. Calculating.
Crushing bones between their teeth.
Was gifted one of the many traits of Death.
Have you ever wondered why the Hyena laughs?
It took Death's voice, left him with silence. They laugh when he is near.
They do not laugh with him. They laugh for him.

What Is This Life?!
by Hortense Bonnet

Plastic was everywhere,
And I had no air.
Was I still alive,
Or with all that plastic I survived?
As soon as I ate food,
I just couldn't conclude.
What did I just devour?
A plastic straw who was not a superpower.
My body didn't move a bit,
And no one was there to remove it.
My eyes were closing,
I was choking.
My peaceful life was coming to an end,
I lost everything like my best friend.
I knew I was dead,
But no one cared.

A Clean Air Solution
by Julia M. Cariello

At first our air was clean
And easy to breathe in.
Now we are less keen
To clean with each passing season.
I just have to wonder why
At least for one day
The factories won't even try
To put their poison air away.
The large cars make smog.
For travel, it's not the best choice.
We could run, bike, or jog
And our world would rejoice.
We can move away from fossil fuel.
Let's find a substitution,
We shouldn't be cruel
We'll find a clean air solution.

Movies
by Jessica Krwawicz

There are many types of movies
Some end happily, others sadly
Some you watch with friends, others with family
They can fill you with horror, or with delight
Some you may admire, others leave you with desire
You can watch them in a theater, or on a couch
While shoveling popcorn inside of your mouth

The Sapphire Sea
by Annelyse Zaccaria

Our beautiful ocean
So bright, so blue;
But what's this commotion
Caused by me, caused by you?
We are polluting the sea,
One of the wonders of Earth.
Crowding waves with debris
Destroying its worth!
To fix this situation
And achieve something great;
We need full participation
Before it's too late.
Let's put our heads together
And devise something new.
Make a change for the better,
So the ocean stays blue!

My Evergreen Tree
by James Freshwater

Outside my home, I see an evergreen tree
Its needles and branches resemble beauty
The tree is a home for many as it stands tall
But trees around me are beginning to fall
Many in the world are being cut down
Instead of a forest there is a town
They are being cut down for things like firewood
But trees cannot be replaced, none of them could
There are so many trees, like maple, dogwood, and oak
That are being cut down for factories causing smoke
Trees help made oxygen and keep the air clean
All trees are important, like my evergreen
So could you help me please
To stop cutting down trees
So don't cut down any tree and be so cruel
And this whole world would be beautiful

Positivity
by George Mirimanyan

Empty fields but filled,
flowing rivers but it sits still,
In the middle of the night, but filled with light,
The people's glass cups are filled to the brim, not half empty,
the sun comes up bright, not gloomy,
step out of that darkness and look into the light,
filled with happiness because happiness is timeless,
it can last forever but it is up to you to decide.

Superhero
by Failyn Locklear

There are people who count on me every day;
I love this place.
I'll never fly away.
Since this is the best space.
Finally found someone like me.
She lights up my whole world;
I think it is meant to be.
Wish she was a superhero with me against the world;
It would be amazing to save the city with her!
Fly all day together
But it's not meant to be,
so I will protect her
forever and ever and ever.
While we are together
I will be her superhero forever.

The Weeping Willow
by Sheera Juricek

Wind whistles through my branches,
carrying on his back words of passion,
words whispered to a lover,
tears cried over the death of a brother.
my leaves rustle in reply,
comforting words, a tired sigh,
emotions roll off me like waves,
talking of my own pains.
my roots burrow deep underground,
as above ground there is not a sound,
the silent hush that winter called,
the quick gasp of one enthralled.
now it's time to sleep until spring,
when once again birds sing,
calling back to life all living things,
asking me to rise and sing with the breeze.

Running
by Brendan Reid

Speeding up, going faster
Accelerating, looking for the finish,
Sweat dripping down, shoes on tight,
One second you're in first, the next you're not,
Reaching for the finish line
The sound of my feet hitting the ground,
Pat, Pat, Pat
And zooming off into the finish line

Kites
by Milena McGowan

Kites come in many shapes and sizes,
Different colors.
Different designs.
They go wherever the wind takes them
Without a care in the world
But there is one thing that holds them back -
A string.
The string only lets them go so far,
No matter where the wind tries to take it.
Sometimes the string comes loose,
But it always seems to become firm once again
But there is hope
For those innocent kites,
A hope that the wind will one day pull hard enough
And set them free forever.

World Hunger
by Gavin Thompson

So you think you know but you have no clue
What if it was different, what if it was you,
A glass of water with a cup of ice
to have what you want, wouldn't that be nice
People walk miles to get something to eat
While we have food right at our feet
We have three meals a day almost every day
Some kids only have one and that's not okay
We have Taco Bell, we have Burger King
While these kids don't have anything
Wouldn't it be nice, wouldn't it be fair
If maybe for once someone would care
So what do we do, what do we say
To the people in charge,
who's going to make this go away?

Mesmerizing Precipitation
by Shaeliyah Clendaniel

A chilling air as the sun sets,
Dark, fluffy clouds slowly begin to distribute icy droplets.
Adding to the plethora of decorations all around,
A calming, yet subtle, whistling sound.
The cool breeze on this breathtaking night,
Icicles glisten in reaction to twinkling lights.
As it snows and snows, each rooftop reveals an even coating,
It is such a pleasing sight,
for the most wonderful time of the year is approaching.

Winter's Tears
by Julia Polycarpe

Winter's coming!
Everyone fears a harsh freeze,
but she's trying to warm up;
why can't they see?
They go inside and don't want to play,
so she stays outside, and cries her pain away.
Winter's tears, she cannot show,
so she turns her tears into snow.
Snow so white, just like cotton;
Her cold exterior is soon forgotten.
They play in the snow,
forgetting their fears,
Little do they know,
they're playing,
In Winter's tears.

Nerves
by Lauren Batuyong

I step on that stage,
and my knees are already shaking.
I pull the mic to my face,
and I feel the noise my breath is making.
I put my feet in place,
take a breath,
and start to sing.
I know my voice is shaky,
but regardless, I keep on going.
Slowly, my nerves are getting to me,
but still, I keep on singing.
My vision is turning blurry,
but the music is still playing, so I keep on singing.
I finish out of breath-
and I can't stop smiling.

Fishing Is My Thing
by Joshua Zdrojewski

What do you want to do today?
Go fishing.
Saturday morning with no chores!
Let's go fishing.
The weather is perfect today.
Maybe I will catch a fish.
Oh no, my rod is bending.
But I still caught the fish.
Tomorrow is another day.
Let's go fishing.

My Life
by Sean DesJardins

Good, happy, sad, bad, evil, smelly, horrible, excellent
We have our ways
It's good, it's bad
That's life so live to your fullest
People hate and love, I'm fine
Rich, poor
Still have feelings and niceness in them
Married, unmarried doesn't matter
Still friends to the end
Have a good day it will help in life
If you don't
Have a good or bad day
Until we meet again
Live life to the fullest

Cherry Petals
by Lydia Ahn

I rustle and wrestle;
The twigs of the branches still hugging onto me
Lovingly; suffocating
I don't want to watch
As the people glare over at the rest of the petals' beauty.
Plucking, picking us bunch by bunch.
Psychotic, as if they didn't have lunch.
My petal twists, wanting to bloom out.
Free,
Like the birds that pass by,
Or the bee in near the garden that flies.
Wishing: hoping
I could travel in the breeze of the wind.
Brisk a touch of the other flowers from my petal tip,
Not having a worry to fall or trip.

The Lake Life
by Gabriella Gordon

The wind whistles gently through the trees.
I canoe through the crystal clear water of the lake.
The water is as calm as a butterfly flying through the bright blue sky.
My oars dance gently across the water.
I glide through the water as swiftly as a swan.
I can see the sand at the bottom.
A fish glides by.
And branches and rocks occasionally sneak up on me from the bottom.
It is calm and beautiful out on the lake.
It is a wonder to behold.

I Swim
by Kyle Sundberg

For 10 years,
I swim in water that is cold.
It is wavy and wild.
I swim like a fish or so I am told.
I dive into the water.
My arms and legs grow bold.
I'm ready to win this.
This feeling will never get old.
I swim across the lane,
As fast as I can.
With no air left and only pain,
I swim like I began.
I swim and touch the wall.
I love to swim most of all.

Sniper
by Jacob Brown

When I played Battlefield 1 for the first time,
it was dark in my basement.
I was ecstatic,
Had my rifle ready for the kill.
The map was colossal.
Put the scope up to my eye, looking for a target.
It was tense and competitive.
Talking to my friend, we were chuckling and talking.
A friendly challenge to see who could get a kill first.
I saw him, an enemy on a horse,
This was my kill,
Took aim and fired.
I killed him.
Ran over and took his horse.

The Field of Choices
by Antonella Ferrari

The fields of pumpkins fill the rolling hills,
through my car window I see the bright orange pumpkin patch,
I walk across the vast field of bright orange pumpkins
they set an orange cast upon the grass,
I walk farther into the immense fields,
I glance up to see a round white pumpkin,
I pick it up feeling the tiny rough bumps that surround it,
when I glance up I notice people staring.
I grab my pumpkin and walk out of the pumpkin patch,
with my head up high with my new pumpkin.

Luna's Message
by Josie Jenkins

The world falls silent,
The time has come.
The day is gone,
What's done is done.
Everyone's asleep,
Their eyes closed tight.
No one ever sees,
My beautiful night.
All the stars and their bright lights
Seem to only shine just out of sight.
As quick as I came,
I now must go.
For day is back;
Hope you enjoyed my show.

Cyberbullied
by Aniyah Alexander

I witnessed something so terrible, something so bad
I knew deep down that the person was sad
Someone so mean, did something so cruel
That they thought it was fun to be rude
They post it up online for the person to see
That when she showed up, everyone thought she was fine
People made fun while the girl sat and cried
The bully walked up and laughed alongside
She ran out of the room, sobbing away
That she ran into a guy leaving the café
I saw her leave, feeling upset
The guy she ran into had been dating the girl who posted on the net
She looked up, staring at him
He walked away, while the lights had dimmed

My Grandmother
by Darragh Buckley

I remember walking up the country road to my grandmother's house
smelling the smoke that came from her fireplace,
and while I'm smelling the smoke,
I can hear her dogs barking in joy, then running to me,
I remember the stories my grandmother would tell me,
when snuggling up beside her on her chair,
I remember all the music she played and the songs she sang,
I remember when we were at a wedding, having all the fun we could ever have,
I remember all the good times I had with her,
I remember my grandmother.

Animals
by Kasey Dugan

Some are big
Some are small
Some are short
Some are tall
Some are soft
Some are rough
Some are sweet
Some are tough
Some have hair
Some have gills
Some live in the sea
Others roam the hills
God created all these creatures
They all belong to one

Imperfect World
by Gabriella Mullakandov

Today know that we live in an imperfect world.
and no one is perfect and always curled.
My friend and I sometimes fight
and maybe some days nothing goes right.
Everything happens for a reason
That we learn and bloom each season.
Today know that we live in a world that can be imperfect.
You will always know you aren't expected to be perfect.
People have mistakes that can never be erased
and some mistakes that can be misplaced.
Mistakes give a strong power
That can always turn into a flower.
Today know that we live in an imperfect world
That can easily be twirled.

Words
by Isabella Godzak

Something, that can make a difference.
Something, that can hurt people.
Something, that can be powerful.
Words.
Used every day, right and wrong.
Used all the time, good and bad.
Words.
Strong, emotional, powerful.
You pick, you choose,
Your words.

Blessed
by Rosie Widmer

Wake up early
Dressing up
Arriving at church
Take the front pew
Kneel
Say my prayers
Receive Him
Through the body and blood
Spending time with Him
Letting Him renew me
Strengthen me
I feel relieved
I feel blessed
Knowing that He loves me

Changes
by Isabella Ochoa

Change is something very important in our lives.
Without change ... everything would stay the same.
What if we always were in winter? We would never be able to enjoy
a nice, smooth, yummy ice cream on a nice, hot, sunny day.
What if we were learning the same thing all over again?
We wouldn't be able to learn something else.
What if we were stuck in one day and had to repeat that day forever?
That would be very boring, because we would do the same thing every day.
But ... what if ... what if we stayed the same age that we are now?
What if we never died? Well never dying sounds awesome,
but staying the same age? That would be terrifying.
We would never be able to explore stuff on our own.
This is why change is very important.
Without change we wouldn't be living in the world that we're in today.

Mist
by Keira Grinstead

Mist swirls around your feet
Mist evaporates in the heat
Up, up, up it goes
Into the clouds,
There it goes!
When it's in the air,
It can spread anywhere.
It can spread
Into the brisk morning air,
Or it can cling to the grass at the fair,
Mist, mist is everywhere!

Jasper
by Andrea Lopez

Divine green eyes used to spy.
Padded paws rough of grey and claws to pry.
With a luscious soft tail to balance if I fail
And a precious pelt mixed with varied hues.
Covered with stripes as black as ink,
Laying above fur as grey as stone,
Along with a belly as white as snow.
A faint padding of steps may be almost unheard
As he roams tonight.
Along with the quiet flutter from a critter.
His ferocious feline gaze locks, as he stalks.
And with a twitch of ears there comes a fatal pounce.
Within a mere second, all is silent.
As he roams tonight.

My Temporary Home
by Tori Cobb

In this camp for over 7 years,
And every day there are new people coming in, hardly ever out.
I ponder,
What would I be doing if I was back in Africa right now?
Only one answer that I could ever think of,
Eating the crops I grew with my family
Singing and dancing with my friends,
Sleeping in my own bed, where I felt safe.
Less than 1% of refugees ever get resettled.
What if I was to be that, 1%.
What if I was to leave this place,
And go back to my own home
and have my old life back.
What if ...?

Bahamas
by John Ferretti

Island surrounded by ocean
Beaches everywhere
Palm trees swaying
Sky vibrant and tropical.
Temperature arid
Water slides to enjoy
Pools to relax in
Dolphins swimming always.
Stingrays swarming
Sounds of waves crashing
Sand under my feet.
So much to explore.

Stop It
by Abby Byers

The tree sways back and forth
Back and forth
Slowly moving
Slowly falling forward
Tipping over to its doom.
Everything moves in slow motion
The leaves, the branches
The sound of chirping birds even sounds delayed
But the only thing standing out unlike the others,
The one sound starring in my nightmares,
Is the sound of a saw cutting down the tree
Why oh why
Did they cut down my home

As Darkness Possesses the Land
by Imad Panjwani

The black stallion gallops into the night,
As darkness possesses the land.
The small chipmunk hides in fright,
While the crab crawls in the sand.
The bear goes into his cave,
While the rabbit ventures to his den.
The wolf seeks meat before he sleeps,
So he sprints in pursuit of a hen.
The hawk flies back to his nest,
After finding worms to eat.
The peacock marvels at her mate's crest,
And so the male's dance repeats.
All these creatures have things to do,
But the rats just gnaw and chew.

Dirtbikes
by Giovanni Valenti

Dirtbikes
Speeding up hitting the gas,
RRRRRRR!!
Accelerating looking for the jump,
Sweat dripping down,
Helmet on tight,
One second you're down, the next you're not,
Speeding through the air,
Reaching for the ramp,
The impact of landing the jump,
And zooming off into the distance
RRRRRRRR!!

Game Day
by Carson Phillips

Put my blue and white on
Leave my house before dawn
Three hours to Happy Valley
Make it for the Blue Band Rally
The sights and sounds of tailgates
Dad starts the grill as we wait
Eat a burger and off we go
Time to see the team put on a show
Find our seats, hear the drum beats
The teams run out
The team wouldn't let us down
Game over, victory bell rings
"The Alma Mater" the team sings

Happy Ending
by Aidan Rodriguez

Not all that glimmers is gold;
But hope.
Not all the shimmers is silver;
But faith.
Hope that the day will come;
A day of glory.
Faith that the day will come;
A day of peace.
A light shines at the end of this dark road,
Cloaking the dark tones of agony.
A light shines at the end of this dark road,
Beaming with colors of happy.
It's a happy ending after all.

Earth
by Ruby Lustig

Oh, Earth, please don't go!
For I was birthed upon your land
And I lay across the sand
You may cause some deaths
But don't take your last breath!
Oh, Earth, you're burning!
Burning and turning-
Into rubble
This causes a lot of trouble
I want your ocean waves hitting my legs
And so please I beg ...
Don't go!

The Secret Garden
by Amelia Longnecker

A place,
Known only in imagination,
Where the roses bloom the brightest,
With a stream trickling through.
Where the trees grow the tallest,
The fruit is the juiciest.
The garden blooms with life.
Light shines through the leaves.
Casting leaf shapes upon the ground,
With long grass that tickles your ankles.
A place where imagination blooms,
Wonder walks a path,
Leading to the secret garden.

Perseverance
by Sienna Steeber

To strive for something so out of sight
To fight with all your might
To set a goal and never give up
To look for the finish line, even when the road is rough
That is tough!
Hard work requires strength.
Strength requires determination at length.
One win at a time ...
It won't be easy when you continually make the climb.
At the end of the tunnel, look for the light.
To get to the light, keep up the fight.
Never stopping with the stress ...
Never-ending hard work determines success!

Fall
by Braden Whitney

Squirrels I don't like,
Annoying, go away now,
Off my bird feeder.

Walls of a House
by Quinn Hechler

I look outside of the bus window at the different houses in the morning
Each one a different shape, size, and story.
I see mansions, the families must be as happy as one could be
But really the parents are fighting and the kids are struggling
On the next corner I see a small broken down house
We come to think the family must be poor and sad
But really the family is grateful and glad
Why do we come to think like this
That money brings happiness
Happiness is a gift we get from the ones around us
The ones we love and the ones we trust
It does not matter about the walls of the house
What is inside the walls is what counts

Where I'm From
by Abigail LoBue

I'm from music and art.
From fun, joy, and laughter that fills up my heart.
I'm from long, stressful nights at the dinner table doing homework.
I'm from Manasquan beach house and fun beach days.
Florida trip, sailing in the bays.
From fun fishing adventures with Popop.
I'm from Mom, an administrative assistant,
Dad, a photographer,
My sister, a high school freshman, and my two dogs, Cutter and Chuckie.
I'm from spending holidays in fun festive ways.
From Thanksgiving at my aunt's.
From family holidays, we love to share.
I'm from clumsy walking and messy talking.
From go outside and ride your bike.
I'm from Grammy's morning pancakes.
And Nanny's homemade pasta sauce.
From Mom's tasty tacos.
I'm from my two yappy dogs, Cutter and Chuckie
From dog hair everywhere,
And to sharing their love with everyone who's there.
I am Abigail Lo Bue

The Math Path
by Megan Chelius

I love math
It's my favorite subject in school
Math is really cool
You start in preschool
unless you're a psychopath

Velvet the Cow
by Peyton Mest

At one time, a little red cow was born
I named her Velvet and our bond of love was so strong
that we didn't need words, we just gazed at each other
And as she grew, I gave her treats of corn and prepared her for the fair
We ran and played in the sun and I rubbed and scratched her with care
And finally the exciting day is here
So I loaded her in the trailer
When we get here, the vet lets her in
and on my cheek I feel a tear of happiness
I love her so much and I can't wait for the show
We get first place, I'm overjoyed
But I knew it since the day she was born that she was an excellent cow
And I can't wait to continue to watch my little red Velvet cupcake grow

Where I'm From
by Aiden Boland

I am from soccer Saturdays,
from football on Sundays.
I am from getting that first sack.
I am from darting across my pool with Nono.
I am from dinner with Nono and Grandma every weekend,
from delicious cookies with Mom.
I am from Dad's homemade burgers,
to tacos on Tuesday.
I am from Mom, an accountant.
I am from Dad, a special needs teacher.
I am from Matthew, a second-grader,
from Teddy, the dog.
I am from Wildwood every August.
I am from traveling to a football game.
I am from going on a family trip to Mexico,
from Aruba with Nono and Grandma.
I am from a chuckle with friends,
to being polite.
I am from helping friends when they need it.
I am from having lots of energy.
I am Aiden Boland!

Dogs
by Spencer Granger

Dogs jump over me
Dogs can be short and skinny
Dogs are heroic

Gray
by Paige Jensen

Floating through the blue
then slowly drifting drab,
trying to distinguish black from blue
causes an everlasting grayish hue.
When your mind goes gray before your hair
and your lungs no longer crave the air,
you'll realize gray isn't that bad
once you start craving a deep, dark, black.

What If
by Ava Dixon

What if we lived in a world where no one was judged,
About their race, color, or size.
What if we lived in a world where climate change didn't exist.
The glaciers aren't melting, temperatures aren't increasing,
and ecosystems weren't destroyed.
What if we lived in a world where no one was poor.
No one had to live on the streets, everyone had clothing,
and not die of starvation.
What if we lived in a world where there was no anger.
We didn't have wars, bullying, and hatred.
What if we lived in a world where no one was racist,
People of different race and color were welcomed anywhere.
What if we lived in a world full of good people,
Everyone had a chance and no one was a bad person.
What if we lived in a world where no one committed suicide
Over depression, bullying, or stress.
What if we lived in a world where there was education everywhere.
The children of Africa could go to school.
But there is no such thing as a perfect world.
Every continent, country, state, county, city, and town
Has flaws, and is never perfect in reality.

Fall
by Autumn St. Hilaire

The leaves fall
When Fall breeze begins
Red, Orange and Yellow leaves
start to blow in the wind
When the Autumn night begins

The Ocean Needs Our Help!
by Alessandra Patti

Pollution is a problem in the ocean.
This creates a big commotion.
Many plants are dying.
This is really terrifying.
Animals in the ocean are getting hurt.
We cannot avert.
They will soon be gone.
We really need to catch on.
Garbage fills the beach.
There is something we need to teach:
Beaches should be pristine,
So all we have to worry about is sunscreen.
Many fish are dying.
We need to start trying
To save the fishes
From our dishes.

The Song of Deforestation
by Isabelle Rae Gurango

I, like many others, love music,
Especially when I am the one making it
From playing piano to playing with a drum stick
I relish in listening, even if the song is not the biggest hit
An instrument I adore is the guitar,
But with all the news of deforestation,
I do not think that they will make it very far.
For guitars are not a need in our nation.
So I say sternly, "Save the trees!"
Save the music industry and its culture,
Listen and hear my pleas!
Do you not see the art in music that may very well be a sculpture?
The banjo and the ukulele, not just the guitar.
Help save all the instruments,
As a world without them would seem bizarre.
Hurry and take action, we must be vigilant.

Snowfall
by Eli Ginsburg

Snowfall
Flakes flutter down
Small hands sip cocoa
Marshmallows swirl sticky on lips
Toasty

Candy
by Jayce Crissy

The air was windy, when I ate some candy.
It was handy when I ate some candy because I have some power.
I named the first bag of candy Andie.
And I named the second bag Mandy.
And I took a picture and it was trendy.

Where I'm From
by Joshua Tweddle

I'm from my dog's heart-melting face
and the cat that tries to scratch me.
From the two cats that end up alongside me,
whenever I need them.
I am from hearing the WAAAH of my baby sister for the first time,
From being stung by bees and wasps,
That arrive in spring and end up nowhere,
From getting sprayed with water guns by my fourth-grade teacher.
I am from falling off the top of a slide and hearing the CRACK of my arm,
From being forced into dressing like a fairy by my sisters,
Feeling oh so embarrassed,
From having the thrill of being on an airplane,
And seeing everything from the sky.
I am from visiting Mamason's house in Florida,
And going on loads of adventures,
From my loving home with affectionate parents,
To my three sisters who either hate me or don't.
I am from Pop Pop's marvelous mashed potatoes,
From Mom's remarkable corn beef and vegetables,
From the smiley face bags from the Chinese takeout.
I am Joshua Tweddle.

Waves of Sweet Songs
by Sofia Kioko

The tide breaks through
The air smells of green slime coming from the ocean
The wind circles from east to west
Gulls treat themselves to whatever creature able to fit in their mouths
And the blue glory continues to crash among others farther out into the sea
Farther and farther in- the waves still rise and drop
Rise and drop.
Rise and drop.
Crash.
Blue and green waters hold more than just weed
From silky orange fish
From the grays of some sharks
From coral that varies
Blue and green waters hold more than just weed
Playful dolphins leap through the air
Restful otters bathe in the sun
Just birthed whales learn from their mothers
A pod of orcas.
A school of fish.
A lone shark.
Waves of sweet songs.

Where I'm From
by Jamie Smith

I am from hanging out with cheerful friends at recess.
From my pleasant 6th grade teachers
I am from a gorgeous autumn day.
From a windy day at the beach.
I am from shopping at the mall.
From being polite to others.
I am from getting my nails done at the nail salon.
From hearing my sister complaining about school.
I am from sledding with cousin on an arctic winter day.
From playing Wiffle ball with my neighbors.
I am from spending time with wonderful family
To going on vacation with them.
Tucker, my dog, jumping on me when I come home from school.
From my cat meowing every night for treats.
I am from going to Ralphs for an Italian Ice.
From going to the Point Pleasant boardwalk.
I am from going to Ocean City, Maryland every summer.
From swimming in my tiny pool.
I am from going on my phone.
From going to my aunt's house to bake.
I am Jamie Smith.

The Hunt Was On
by Madison Osborne

The Hunt Was On
We were all excited.
While looking at the colors surrounding us,
in our classroom.
The Hunt Was On.
We were ready to start.
"Ready. Set. GO!"
The Hunt Was On.
There were a lot of egg.
We were collecting them fast,
so now they were near gone.
The Hunt Was On.
One egg left.
We looked for the egg.
We could tell we were getting close,
as if it was under our noses.
The egg was found.
The Hunt Was Over.
We were having such a blast.
But we had to stop and wonder,
who had done the best.

Emotions
by Morgan Osborne

Emotions
Out of nowhere came The conversation,
"We don't want to make the decision without you,
But-
It's happening if you guys are ok."
"We're moving!"
"Yay!" We are all excited,
It's going down fast,
But, in the blink of an eye-
BLINK
Just two weeks left!
It finally hit me,
Emotions-
One day I'm happy, the next I'm sad-
I'm moving away from everyone!
My cousins-
My friends-
My family-
I'm leaving everyone behind!
I'm getting eaten alive!
Emotions-

Where I'm From
by Ryan Settle

I am from Mom's magic peanut butter cookies,
From Grandma's great cake.
I am from Grandma's great French toast on Christmas morning,
From Red Oak.
I am from playing with my sister,
From Mom being a nurse.
I am from being a big brother,
From Halloween with family.
I am from watching action movies with my grandfather,
From helping my great grandfather when he needs it.
I am from wrestling,
From playing tackle football.
I am from going to Myrtle Beach, South Carolina,
From my dog, Zoey.
I am from new shoes,
From new clothes.
I am from Mrs. Burns,
From Ms. Wolkom.
I am from Mrs. Grabowski, my third-grade teacher,
From Mrs. Scarfi, who I share a birthday with.
I am Ryan Settle

Help Me
by Leah Pakan

Dear God, it's Thursday
I don't think I'm gonna make it 'cause I just can't shake it
She trying to break me but I just can't, I'm trying to find another way around that
I cannot take this crap, I really can't
I need help, dear God, please help
She's hitting me and slapping me as hard as she can
while other kids are getting as much as they can
My opinion's always wrong, it's never right
Try having a conversation with her, you'll just fight
The only place I've ever known was my room
where I spent hours crying 'cause there's nothing else to do
I love her, I really do, but sometimes loving someone can hurt you
She sees me more as a servant than a daughter
If my dreams were a reality then I'd have a father.
But he left her, left me, left us lonely
No food, no water, just us dying
Poor to the cent, nothing made sense
How you supposed to love if you never felt it?
How you supposed to talk if you never spoken?
It's the little things that matter to me,
so dear God, if you can help out that would be lovely

Never Coming Back
by Kensley Harris

I lost you when I was eight
Never to come back
You left as fast as the wind
Finding your own path through the empty void of death,
You were forced to leave,
But happy to go,
It ended your suffering.
It eased the pain,
No longer to be felt,
But always remembered by the ones who loved you most.
As you left you looked peaceful,
With your muzzle in the slightest smile
and your face softened without any lines of pain.
We wept and we mourned
For you, our pet that departed across the bridge of clouds,
That separates the living and dead
Now the empty space that you left in my heart,
Can never be filled since it tore me apart.
I miss you still, four years after,
With hopes that one day we'll find each other,
For you left me vulnerable to the heartache that I surrendered to for so long.

I See His Face
by Eva Ginsburg

Every time I see his face it brings a smile to mine
He embraces me with open arms
I feel the warmth of his cozy flannel shirt
Hearing him chuckle at my jokes warms my heart and fills it with joy
Ever since he was a teacher his eagerness for teaching and learning never stopped
Whenever I see him, or even if I don't,
I will always be learning new things from him every day
Whether it is a new fact, discovery, or even a lesson learned
We go fishing off the dock
Waiting patiently for a tug on the line
I feel a pull
I reeled in an old shoe
Before I know it we both start laughing with silliness
One of his best qualities is his kind, gentle heart
and unconditional love for his family
My younger brother and I wish to grow up just like him
Hopefully filling his shoes but not like the smelly one we found fishing
I ring his doorbell or as I dream it at night
My eyes well up with tears
I see his face
It is my grandpa

Horse
by Nathan Beecher

Horse
Soft, friendly
Running, cantering, galloping
Loveable when you are sad
Colt

Happy Holidays
by Lauren Zehner

A fresh blanket of chalky white snow
Coats the ground with a sparkling glow.
People are getting excited,
Everyone seems delighted.
Selecting a pine colored Christmas tree
Fills my body with eagerness and glee.
Decorating is our favorite part,
That is when the magic starts.
The toasty and restful fire is bright,
It will keep us in high spirits tonight.
As we all gather near,
We realize the magic of Christmas cheer.

Where I Am From
by Justin Sclavunos

I am from my loving mom,
my awesome dad,
and my clumsy brother.
I am from my grammy's welcoming living room,
and my uncle's vacation home.
I am from my two cute cats, Chloe and Jinxy.
I am from my Holland Lop bunny, Boo,
my three fish, Goldie, Barney, and Elmo,
and my old cat, Tiara.
I am from the sunny scorching baseball fields,
and the wood planks on the basketball court.
From my backyard where we play tackle football,
and fanatical football Sundays.
I am from World Series wars with my dad for money.
I am from my dad getting attacked by a raccoon out of the garbage can,
and getting body slammed by my brother in the bright white snow.
From jumping into a wave and getting knocked over,
and doing my first backflip into the warm pool.
I am from helping people,
to being kind.
I am Justin Sclavunos

Basketball
by David Makowka

There once was a boy that was small
He wanted to play basketball
He wasn't the best
And he hurt his chest
So maybe he wouldn't play after all.

Green
by Gabriella Harrison

What is green?
This is what I mean,
Leaves on a tree,
The inside of a kiwi,
Emeralds in a ring,
A frog in a spring.
Seaweed in the ocean,
Causing a commotion.
Green beans in a garden,
Ready to be frozen.
Grass on a hill,
Where I can lay and chill.
Chalkboards in school,
Broccoli that makes me full.
As you can clearly see
This is green to me.

Soldier
by Ava Heaton

When I kissed his cheek,
I knew it would be the last.
He was helpless,
But still having a blast.
He was strong.
Always had a smile on his face.
He loved me forever.
He was going to a better place.
I cried a lot,
When the time finally came.
He was an incredible man,
It truly was a shame.
He wasn't just a great soldier,
No, not at all
He was the best grandfather,
Who would never let me fall.

Caterpillar
by Brett Fetter

I watched as a caterpillar crawled along my patio to get some leaves.
As the caterpillar ate the leaves, it got fatter and fatter until it was full.
As it crawled to a leaf on a bush, he morphed into a cocoon.
In 8 hours or so, he hatched out into a pretty butterfly
with colors so bright you could have seen them from a mile.

Withering Home
by Isabella Arevalo-Lis

Our Earth is slowly dying,
because there is so much pollution in the air.
It is as if we are not even trying,
I just do not think that it is fair.
There are more eruptions,
more burning sunrays,
more consumption,
and more water in the bays.
Help our trees
because they're on fire.
There are also the bees,
who are not fine.
Clean our oceans,
our corals.
We really do not need a commotion
because it will cleanse our morals.

Save the Ocean
by Giacomo Imperiale

In the ocean don't throw things away
It won't bother you but the animals will pay
The fish just can't leave the ocean
That will cause such a commotion
Do not just say it's really ok
The fish must live with that garbage every day
While we're at it, let's talk about coral
Because it cannot be very oral
It's dying and bleaching our beautiful sea
And now you ask, "How could this be?"
It's the temperature rising high like the sky
Now I'm even saying Oh My!
At a high rate the ocean is rising
This might seem very surprising
Now that you know what to do and what not
Please take care of our ocean and love it a lot.

Nothing
by Jennifer Bensley

Write a poem, they say,
Help me find the words, I pray.
Write what's on your mind,
Nothing, nothing at all I find.
So I find myself writing this,
This poem full of emptiness.
Write what's on your mind,
Nothing, nothing at all I find.

Seize the Day
by Hafsah Raza

Seize the day as they say
Which you can do in so many ways
You could seize the day in a pool
Or just try to be really cool
Or you could seize the day by playing ball
Or just give your best friend a call
As you can see there are so many ways to seize the day
So I dare you to try every single one today!

Where I'm From
by Anthony Barone

I am from Mom, Dad, and Lea,
From my soft and furry cat named Oreo.
I am from Grandma and Grandpa.
I am from every taco Tuesday,
I am from Mom's crispy bacon.
I am from juicy bacon cheeseburgers.
I am from a yearly vacation to Grandma and Grandpa's.
I am from traveling with my soccer, basketball, and baseball teams,
And hanging out with everybody while I am there.
I am from the booming sound of the basketball,
While beating the best team as the worst team,
In the competitive basketball playoffs.
I am from the fluffy grass of the soccer fields.
I am from getting furious at the Giants.
I am from my Super Bowl party,
And having fun while we play.
I am from school,
And helping others.
I am from including everybody in our games,
And helping others when they are disappointed.
I am Anthony Barone

The Song of the Forest
by Abby Peden

Every evening when the moon comes out
And the wind starts to blow,
The forest is brought to new life in moonlight
And they shall begin their song.
The trees start to sway
And the flowers toss and turn.
The crickets start to chirp along
While the birds provide the tune.
The squirrels and chipmunks chatter
Inside their hollowed homes
As they cry out the verses
To their timeless woodland song.
The animals get ready for sleep
As they sing the refrain,
And the trees all dance together
As their leaves glimmer in the moonlight.
The wind then stops blowing
And the trees are perfectly still.
One by one, the animals rest in perfect slumber
And the song comes to an end.

Where I'm From
by Morgan Rafferty

I am from the smell of freshly painted soccer lines,
from the smell of chalk in the rock gym.
I am from soccer Sundays with Dad,
from the roaring soccer fans.
I am from arm wrestling amazements,
to perfect plank competitions.
I am from the pain of holding a 6 minute plank,
from beating the boys.
I am from Mom, a human resources managing director.
I am from Dad, an insurance executive.
I am from Clanagh, a third grader and my best friend.
I am from climbing on slippery rocks with Uncle Neil,
From D.C. adventures with Mom.
I am from school days with Granny, from going to the stores with Pop
I am from visits to Granny and Granda's house.
I am from Dad who always encourages me and helps me with soccer,
and tells me that I'm a soccer god.
I am from being caring and helpful,
from a determined mindset.
I am from never giving up when things get tough.
I am Morgan Rafferty!

Fall
by Cameron Chapman

Fall comes around
It gets cooler
Wind blowing trees
Beautiful leaves falling
A blend of red and orange
Summer is leaving
A new chapter in our lives
A new school year
Long pants and jackets
Football and soccer
Candy and costumes
Jumping in leaves and puddles
But soon we will be inside
It will get colder
Playing basketball inside
Sitting by the fire drinking hot chocolate
Red and green
Presents and Christmas
Snowy days and stay home days
Winter is coming

Hidden Heroes
by Willow Phelps

My teacher wants a computer.
For that is why, I'm writing a poem
But NO poem can describe my teacher
So now I will attempt to show the world,
Why we need teachers like mine
We grow
We learn
We laugh
We inspire
She tells us to read
Even though we may not want to,
We eventually get the best experience
From a book, in our lives
She tells us stories,
Ruth, the man in the well, Etc.
And even though we may not realize it, but these stories change us
And that's some reasons why
We all need
A hero
Like mine

Seasons
by Alana Mitchell

When the ground turns white
When the days grow cold
When you see your breath
Winter is here
When the snow goes
When the flowers bloom and blossom
When the weather is rainy
You know Spring is here
When school lets out
When the sun burns
And the ice cream churns
Yay! Summer is here
When the last leaves turn brown and fall
When the heat goes down
And when school starts again
We all know Autumn is here
But no matter the weather
No matter the season
All year round
Fun is here

Where I'm From
by Daniel Camacho

I'm from the first time on a plane,
To being on a plane alone, and going to Mexico to meet relatives.
I'm from going to Pennsylvania,
to going to Orlando, Florida.
I am from driving my miniature jeep,
from playing random notes on the piano.
I am from touching a steamy iron,
from feeling blue on my birthday.
I am from eating homemade hominy,
from eating Houlihan's nachos.
I am from eating marvelous mango ice at Rita's,
From drinking a strawberry smoothie at Dairy Queen
From liking Costco churros.
I am from my parents confessing I was eating fish instead of chicken,
From meeting my grandparents for the first time.
I am from my aunt cheering me up
from meeting my great grandparents for the first time in Mexico.
I am from being an only lonely child
To being bilingual
And being funny and kind.
I am Daniel Camacho

The Lake
by Lily Shahan

Toward the dock
Onto the boat
Down the ladder
Within the frigid water
My family is afloat.
Through the ropes
Under the water
Away from the shore
Against the rafts
I swim carelessly.
On top of the tube
Above the water
Over the waves
In back of the boat
I speed across the water.
Away from the dock
Back over the hill,
To the car
Over the bridge
I drive back to the cabin.

Second Grade
by Raymond Coles

Second grade,
Pokémon cards banned!
No trading,
My binder in my desk,
Cards inside,
Make a plan, look through the cards,
Set up my deck.
Planning my win,
Hands in my desk.
Didn't notice she was passing me,
She looks at my desk.
"Raymond?"
My reflex reaction was to push them into my desk.
"Give me your cards!"
"Ok," as I took some of the cards,
And gave them to her
With the rest ... the rest I secretly,
Stashed in the back wall of my desk,
She thought she had them all.
I'm so sorry Mrs. T.

Preposterous Pollution
by Lena Norelli

The ocean, the sea
So beautiful and free
Glistening by the shore
That's how it was before
Now machines and reservoirs
Burst oil from the ocean floor
This fills the immense ocean
With many terrible types of potions
Then people tend to litter trash
Do they realize that they thrash
Contemporary organisms just like them
Are we so amazing then?
Why do humans always say
"We'll fix it," but don't, anyway
If we lived in the polluted sea
Then we would no longer be
Pollution really has to stop
Or wondrous sea life will soon drop
To the extensive ocean floor
Breathing ... not anymore

Not But So Long Ago
by Simone Valentine

Not but so long ago
The sky would cry as the winds would blow
Many creatures would freely walk around
Until we came and tore up the ground
We need nature to survive
Yet we act like we're in overdrive
Why must we chop down the trees
Don't they give us a clean breeze
So many species we never got to understand
Because we are too busy taking over their land
Greed took over who's got the most or the best
And we haven't shed a thought for that bird in its nest
We all need to reduce our waste
Let's do it now with a bit of haste
Global warming and greenhouse gases
To recognize the damage you don't need glasses
Our world is constantly changing
Constantly rearranging
How much longer until we know
How much longer until this world decides to blow

Let's Save the Trees
by Bobby Canada

I love the trees
For they provide paper
They hold many bees
Do not be a taker
They give out air
But many cut them down
Plant more if you dare
Before they fall to the ground
They hold many birds
They can help make a book
They hold our thoughts and words
They can change our outlook
So help save the trees
For they do much good
I beg you, please
Save them if you could

Where I'm From
by Connor Lee

I'm from Morgan, Mom, and Dad,
From Poppop and Grandma.
I am from my mom, a special needs teacher,
From my dad who is a P.E. teacher.
I am from my four guinea pigs, Holly, Cocoa, Cupid, Spencer,
From my dog, Docker,
And my two hermit crabs, Martin and Cooper.
I am from Ocean City, Maryland every year,
From Florida every other year.
From hearing the splash when jumping off a waterfall in Tennessee,
I am from going up the arch in Missouri.
I am from being competitive and never giving up,
From being funny and always making people laugh.
I am from being honest and never letting people down.
I am from squishy dark green mats at the dojo,
From the smell of the wet soccer fields.
From hearing the crack of the bat at the top deck of the Yankee game.
From chasing a petite dog for my underwear.
I am from the hard brown boards at the Keansburg Boardwalk,
I am from binging the galactic glories of Star Wars with Dad.
I am Connor Lee

Winter
by Chloe Wright

Hot chocolate steaming hot
While the kids laugh outside,
When they come inside
They have to get ready to say goodbye,
The next morning the snow is blowing
Wilder than the car horns are agoing.
When the snow stops blowing,
The kids make a snowman
While making the levels, a kid knocks it down
And says, oh no man.
Flour, sugar, and butter creamed together in a bowl
Mixed with yolk, milk, and vanilla, it is accidental coal
Candy canes and hot chocolate, everyone whines
While stirring the hot chocolate with candy canes, it decides to bind
Waiting for Santa is getting harder with such a joy,
Kids wondering, am I even getting a toy?
The last sledding was such a blast,
I always wonder why does it end so fast!
Winter's leaving as Spring is coming,
I can't wait to hear thunder rumbling

The Night Life
by Lily Galietta

The stars glow bright in the sky,
Twinkling as they shine down on the earth.
As you walk alone in the darkness smiling up at the moon,
You hear a sudden rustling in the treetops.
You look up into the leaves
And you can see the dark shape of an owl.
Looking at you with curiosity,
You smile and wink at the bird
Then continue on quietly.
As you're walking along your all too familiar trail,
You stop to see an opossum who just happens to be there,
The opossum is startled to see you
And plays dead.
Eventually he gets up and moves on as you do.
A nightingale quickly passes in the night sky.
Now, you knowing all the night myths,
Legends and tales, is quick to prevail,
Only means of good times when you reach your destination,
Campfire and s'mores with friends await your arrival, you think and smile!
How glorious is the nightlife!

Friendship
by Gitty Fried

I have friends by my side every day,
They are nice to me in every way,
We are together all the time,
We even write poems that rhyme,
Friends are amazing, friends are cool,
You meet them while you're in school,
Friends in the summer, friends in the fall,
In the spring we play ball,
My friends are sweet, nice and caring,
And of course, they're always sharing,
Whenever I am feeling sad,
My friends help me to feel glad,
I'm always with friends and I'm never alone,
We like to do our homework over the phone,
My friends are absolutely the best,
They are really better than the rest!!

Where I'm From
by Alex Iglesias

I am from boisterous basketball courts,
from game nights with Meema and Papa.
I am from being attacked by wacky raccoons,
from hanging out with my baffling baby cousins.
I am from zipping ziplines in Costa Rica,
from getting lost in mischievous mirror mazes.
to nutty Nerf wars with my cousins.
I am from precious pizza pizzazz from Basille's,
from Popeyes crispy crunchy chicken.
I am from delicious donuts from Dunkin' Donuts.
I am from fabulous football Sundays,
from New Years at Hershey.
I am from marvelous monkey bread on Christmas mornings,
to rapidly gobbling down Aunt Nicki's heavenly cookies.
I am from a beautiful, cozy house,
from a great, loving family.
I am from the family dogs, Henny, Remi, and Mia.
I am from Dad, a military man,
from Mom, an amazing caring mother.
I am from Andrew, my brother.
I am Alex Iglesias.

The Cold, Dark Night
by Abigail Breakiron

The day is ending.
The day is done.
We kiss goodbye
The warm, bright sun.
Once so close,
Once held so tight,
But now we meet
With the cold, dark night.
Introducing bright stars,
Introducing the white moon.
It showers us with things
We once thought were our doom.
But now it is known,
What the darkness holds.
The story it tells,
And how that story unfolds.
Comforting and soft,
Is the dim, dark sky.
The trees hum and sway
As the chilly winds sigh.

Yes
by Miah Sabo

The word that starts the best things in life,
a word of new beginnings,
an adventure waiting to happen.
YES.
3 letters that can turn the tide in your life
3 letters that open new doors
3 letters. That's it. That's all you have to say.
YES.
the best things in life start with yes.
1 little word opens so many doors.
say it more often, wear it out.
YES.
YES, allows you to follow your dreams,
YES, allows you to become the best version of yourself,
YES, brings out the best in life.
YES.
take my word for it, yes is a good word,
the best things in history started with yes, use it to write your own history
without a doubt say YES, make your story great
YES.

The Fall
by Michal Sheps

The leaves are changing colors,
Some yellow, some orange, some brown.
A few are multi-colored,
They're scattered all over the ground.
I stroll outside, it's getting colder,
The air's so fresh and crisp.
The seasons are changing now I say,
As I blow the summer a kiss.
I look at the beautiful scenery,
And breathe some fresh air through my nose.
I spot a squirrel gathering acorns,
And watch the birds flying high and low.
I think fall is a wonderful season,
Full of spectacular sights for miles and miles.
I can't wait for more leaves to fall down,
And make lots of colorful leaf piles.

Where I'm From
by Steven Russo

I'm from the black grim turf on the soccer fields,
I'm from getting transferred to an elite soccer academy team.
I'm from the soccer cones
I'm from the pure white soccer net in my backyard.
I'm from my mom's savory crispy fried chicken recipe with salt and pepper,
to dim sum and getting hot peppery Chinese food
I'm from the extra cheddar goldfish packs.
I'm from a charismatic personality,
to helping others.
I'm from not discriminating a person's skin color,
to a home full of laughter.
I'm from diving into the roaring salty waves at Myrtle Beach.
I'm from traveling to the aqua blue water park.
to my grandpa's wooden cabin in the woods.
I'm from a bright green soccer ball in my backyard to the store Zara.
I'm from writing my feelings out when I'm bored,
to Grandma calling me to wish me a Happy Birthday.
I'm from my dog pooping in my upstairs bathroom floor.
I'm from my dog taking shoes under the dining room table.
I'm from my dog singing Happy Birthday.
I'm Steven Russo!

Rock
by Michael Allen

There was a kid who ate a rock.
When he swallowed it down, he left everyone in shock.
He said it tasted like a bear
He asked if anyone would like to share
When he was full, he stuffed the rest in a sock.

Simple, Yet Complicated
by Julia Grodensky

Complication has always been quite Simple
As Simplicity has always been Complicated in some way
And forever will it be so.
If somethings seems too Simple, it is more Complicated than that
If it is too Complicated, it is Simple.
You are ... Simply ... Overthinking.
If everything in life was too Simple, where would the teachers teach,
or the learners learn,
or the World be Fun?
Yet, if everything was too Complicated, the teachers wouldn't teach,
Nor would the learners learn,
And the World would be without fun.
No more adventure.
The concept of this is quite simple.
Simple is Complicated, Complication is Simple.
And forever will it be so.

Where I'm From
by Adrianna Johnson

I am from my funny dad, to my nice mom.
From my heart-warming poppy, to my helpful nanny.
From my cool aunt, to my crazy uncles.
I am from my hoping of being a doctor
at St. Jude Children's Research Hospital.
I am from my mom's hot and cheesy mac and cheese bowl
to her spicy buffalo wings.
From her juicy tacos to her chicken cutlets.
I am from my comfortable cheer shorts to my sports tops.
From my fancy uniform to my fancy bows.
I am from my many different color sweatshirts to my gold tank tops.
I am from my cheetah pants to my white shoes.
I am from my mom about to have a baby.
From wanting to be a mom when I am older.
I am from my sixth grade teachers, Ms. Wolkom and Mrs. Burns.
I am Adrianna Johnson.

The Mask
by Bella Pillittere

With it on they smile,
With it off they turn away.
All I let show is the painted smile
To cover my tears.
To cover the hole.
Inside I feel pain,
But I don't let it show.
All I show is a
Plastered grin.
A plastered laugh.
But The Mask
Covers the sorrow.

In a Book
by Chayalla Katz

In a book, there are pages
In the pages, there are words
In the words, there is history
In the history, there is adventure
In the adventure, there is friendship
In the friendship, there is betrayal
In the betrayal, there is loyalty
In the loyalty, there is hope
In the hope, there is a dream
In the dream, there are wishes
In the wishes, there is success
That is in a book

Camping
by Mitch Stroup

It is hard to not get lost in nature's beauty.
Everyday problems fade away.
Boredom from bland routines
Supplemented with excitement.
Adventure is in everything.
Life lessons and camping skills can be learned.
It's hard to be gloomy because it's such a positive experience.
There is never a dull moment.
Campers must respect nature to keep camping possible.
It's always disappointing to leave.
People often say "back to reality."
It is so amazing it does feel like a fantasy world.

Spring Has Sprung
by Keeley Sniadach

Spring is almost here
Pretty flowers are coming
They smell delightful

The Boy
by James Andrews

There once was a boy filled with joy.
Nothing bad could make him mad or sad.
He knew that everybody had a warm spot in their heart.
Every bully thought he was soft, so they picked on him a lot.
The boy stopped the bullying once and for all.

Erasers
by Natalie Macnow

Some of us are hard,
Some of us are tough.
Some of us are easy to be used,
Some of us are useful.
Sometimes we are needed,
Sometimes we are not.
We are just like erasers,
Most people just don't see it.

Where I'm From
by James Galizia

I am from my grandma's miraculous mashed potatoes
I am from my great grandma's marvelous macaroni
I'm from my grandma's sensational scrambled eggs
I'm from my mom's perfect pancakes
I'm from playing with my great grandpa
I'm from racing my dad in the backyard
I'm from having bike races with my cousins
I'm from playing videos games all night with my cousins
I'm from losing my favorite dog, Bear
I'm from hearing the first meow of my first pet cat
I'm from nursing a bird with a broken leg with my mom
I'm from hearing the *woof* of my grandma's new dog
I'm from putting up Christmas decorations with my dad
I'm from getting "matching" costumes with my baby sister on Halloween
I'm from putting the star on the Christmas tree and being on a ladder shivering
I am James Galizia

A Birthday Poem
by Delana Duncan

Your Birthday is here,
Getting old is no fun,
But don't fret or fear;
You'll still be Number One!
Whether it be rain or snow,
Sleet or ice, sunny or no,
I hope your birthday
Will still be nice!

A Rainy Day
by Jayla Peterson

Sitting by the fire while it's pouring down rain
Drip, drop, drip, drop down the drain
In the house
I stay as quiet as a mouse
Yet, all the books I read
Now I'm ready for bed
All curled up in my blanket I say
Oh why such a rainy day?

Family
by Nicole Tejeda

One of the most important things
Every person has and is apart of, is a family.
Family is not only by blood, if not
Is also the ones around you and the ones you love.
A home is not your family.
A home is Where your family dwells in.
A family is not to be ignored.
A family is supposed to encourage, help, and love you.

Don't Know Where To Go
by Alex Peryea

The trees are flowing, the grass is growing,
All the animals are getting going,
All the people are going around, getting around,
But nobody knows where we are going,
We are all just flowing with what happens.
We wish to know where we go in life,
but a lot of us don't know where we go in life
The answer is Jesus Christ

The Boogeyman and His Van
by RJ Buscher

There once was an old and pale man,
Who was driving in a pink van.
Then he hit the brake,
For he ran into a rake.
He then became the boogeyman.

Friends
by Ethan Yakubov

Friends at school!
Friends at school can play and share.
Friends at school are kind and fair.
Friends at school will always be there for you.
Friends at school will always support you.
Friends at school are big and small.
Friends at school are the best of all!

Where I'm From
by Sadie Cizin

I'm from bows in my hair
To ballet dancing after school
From twirling a spinning baton
I'm from sunny days at the beach.
From blazing warm days at Grandma's pool
I'm from fun-filled day trips and many more.
I'm from baking amazing cakes with Great Nana.
To Romeo's hot crispy pizza
I'm from Polar Bear's hot fudge brownie sundae
And spectacular Christmas cookies made with love.
I'm from hot sunny Wildwood days
To the annual grand Thanksgiving in Hershey Park
I'm from memorable road trips across the country.
I'm from my mom, a teacher
My dad, a federal agent
I'm from my crazy brother, Jack John the Leprechaun.
My sister, Sabrina.
I'm from helping my siblings
I'm from being considerate,
helpful, friendly, and forgiving
I'm from friends and family.
I am Sadie Cizin

Siblings
by Erik Lorenzo

Brothers and Sisters
they fight all light
and all the night
they forgive and forget
and they love all life peacefully

Cherry Blossoms
by Jaylee Duncan

When all the Cherry Blossoms bloom
And the sun lights up my quiet room
The April showers
Bring May flowers
And I'll know Spring's coming soon.

Cats
by Reyna Borrello

Cats can come in many colors
But not red, green, or blue.
Their coats are like crayons in a box,
Except you dropped a few.
The markings on the coats can be described as
A painter gone askew
Striped, spotted, and speckled
As the animals in a zoo.
You can buy expensive toys
But what good would that do,
When they prefer to chase around
The mop and your left shoe.
If you are sitting on your chair
They will sit on your lap
And cozy themselves up
For a nice evening nap.
As you fall asleep
And your dreams start to stir
You can feel the low rumble
Of a little cat's purr.

The Forest
by Regina Torrance

Glowing stars dancing in the light
Cascading through the barrier causes them to ignite.
Motes twirl like a ballerina in the center light.
The sea of woven branches fills the horizon with an ombre of jade.
The canopy covers the floor with a shadow
Only speckled streams of light can break.
A sudden rhythmic beat starts within the feet of a strange passerby.
If they are to fly then they sway with the wind and sky.
The autumn breeze shuffles the leaves
Causing the endless barrier to ripple.
Light flutters with the blanket
Causing amber stars to tumble to the ground.

A Midnight Dream
by Kiera Bolkovich

Once upon a midnight dream, my head's aching, my body's weary
Pillows and blankets piled up high with my soft sheets in the floor.
Longing to go back and lay down, standing in my doorway dreaming,
As I'm about to leave there is a sudden knock at my door,
I heard my mom say, "Get up now! I won't tell you this no more!"
"Okay," I said, further more
I went out the door as my face started to pour,
Oh how I wish I was back home dreaming, dreaming, nothing more.
I had to walk my way to school instead of waking up in a pool of drool.
Sitting in class as tired as can be, my teacher starts to bore,
I stood up and said, "I can't take this anymore!"
Running out the door coming home to my soft sheets on the floor.

Equity
by Allaina Brown

The quality of the dream about equality is short and lean.
If I believe in something that has never been seen.
If I put trust or faith that no one sees.
If I have a wider pelvis but in my mind
I feel like I should be a guy on the outside
If I'm attracted to the same side, that type of love is denied,
we're supposedly misguided
The pigment of my skin shouldn't give you a right to judge
but if I'm a black guy and pulled the trigger to the cop,
doesn't he have a right to shoot
Now who's in the wrong
But I hope one day we'll live in peace but I guess that's only my dream.

The Ocean
by Caroline Fannon

The waves hug my feet
Splash! Splash! Huge waves rolling in
A Beautiful Day

Winter Is Here
by Beatrice Musto

When weather gets so harsh that the cold feels like bites!
You go inside and watch your whole town go white!
You can make some homemade sugar cookies.
Then go to some Christmas parties!
Go find the best tree and hop to an exit.
Add ornaments and a star so Santa can leave presents!
We put up some decorative holiday lights!
"Hey who threw that? Snowball fight!"
You change into layers and go downtown for sledding!
As you slide down the hill you wonder, "Which way am I heading?"
Come all covered in snow and family said, "Oh dear!"
And all you can say with a sigh, "Winter is here."

Where I'm From
by Joe Imbriano

I am from New Jersey
I'm from my mom's Steak Sundays.
I am from Taco Tuesday. I am from funnel cake Friday.
I am from Macaroni Monday.
I am from French toast Friday.
I am from making and baking Mondays.
I am from Fitness Friday.
I am from Tracking Tuesday.
I am from wall ball Wednesdays.
I am from riding bikes with boys.
I am from Soccer Saturdays.
I am from Football Friday.
I am from Friend Friday.
From walking dog Wednesday.
From Star Wars Sunday.
From Saturday Scary movies.
From Picture Perfect.
I am from Superhero Saturday.
From funny movies Friday.
From food shopping Friday.
I am Joe Imbriano

Invisible Van Gogh
by Maya Clough

My pencil
Is better than any paintbrush.
It paints emotions, and concepts
And every other invisible thing.
My pencil is like a shovel,
My paper sand,
My poem a sandcastle,
And my eraser the tide.
Washing it all away,
So I may start once again.
Except, I make sandcastles of dungeons
And dragons with girls
Locked in towers
And then get scolded
Because they wanted to see castles
With bows and ribbons,
But not the truth,
Never the truth
So my sandcastles are made in dessert
Where they will never be found

Long Ago
by Madelyn Hamilton

Long ago
When faeries sang and mermaids frolicked
A land of magic slowly died
Long ago
When cavemen bruted and dinosaurs reigned
A land of stone slowly died
Long ago
When kings ruled and damsels distressed
A land of castles slowly died
Long ago
When explorers mapped and natives fled
A land of adventure slowly died
Right now
When computers steal our days away
And we trust our phones more than our friends
We are in an era of mass production
We best mountains every day
But what is it all for?
Do we make them proud?
The ones from long ago?

Special Spring
by Rabiya Najim

It blooms every year,
It shows its clear,
Colorful plants,
With hot pants,
Seeing the flowers,
For hours,
Hearing birds chirping,
And cold ice slurping,
Kids play
With clay,
Next spring awaits,
With plates,
On tables,
With colorful cables,
Oh spring,
You always bring the king to the throne,
Like it's his zone,
Next time we wait,
It'll be like a date,
With debate.

Dancing In the Rain
by Ainsley Bigelow

There is a woman
Dancing in the rain;
On the busy sidewalk,
Meticulously and gracefully weaving around people.
The other civilians,
Hurriedly moving towards refuge,
Seem oblivious to this leaping figure.
Her robust, yet elegant frame,
Splashes the puddles,
Making rainbows in the water from the light.
Her ebullience radiates from every motion of her body;
Such a contrast from the others,
Hustling to escape the rain.
My heart beats
With every thump of her landing feet.
I know this woman,
Dancing in the rain,
Is not a figment of my imagination
As much as
The person I aspire to be.

The Endless Shot
by Aryel Sealey

Chapter one
I'm off to the doctor to get a shot
They prick me just above the elbow
It hurts so I cry and cry
My mom tells me that it's going to be alright
Chapter two
Going to the doctor next week to get another shot
They prick me again
So I cry
My mom tells me that it will be alright
Chapter three
Why am I here again?
I've already gotten two, why another?
My mom doesn't tell me anything
Chapter four
I'm sick and tired of it all
So I don't cry
My mom isn't there
Chapter five
I don't show up

Bed of Grass
by Kelly Miller

Beyond the waves, beyond the plains
I lay in a bed of grass
Across the sea, across the fields
You sit in a tree, thinking of me
I take a breath, so do you
It seemed like we stuck like glue
But the glue wore away
And you got shipped away
I only await the day when you lay with me
On this bed of grass full of memories
But then ...
The grass died on either side of me
I heard a snapping, so did you
You tried to climb or grab anything you could
Call for help, but nothing came, so you fell back
And drifted off thinking of the bed of grass
You hoped we would one day share
The tree branch fell
So did you, and that's the day
My heart tore in two.

Walking Til I Hear No Sound
by Abigail Swiderski

Walking 'til I hear no sound
The crunch of leaves fades away
My feet are stuck to the grimy ground
Trying to get people to stay
I wait here 'til my passing
Asking for a hand
But this torture is forever lasting
And I become one with the land
Stopping the time, turning it back
Waiting for this to stop
Finding something I still lack
Waiting for the big hand to drop.
Patience, the answer to all
Well, the answer to all but one
My problems are starting to look small
So my whining is done.
My future, my presence, my past
All crumbling down
Cannot escape from the life that will forever last
And in the dirt I drown.

No One Knows
by Annabella Sottile

No one knows how I feel.
No one knows what I do.
No one knows what I think.
No one knows the truth.
Everyone always assumes things.
People always spread false rumors.
No one has the time to get to know me.
No one really cares how I feel about that.
They're always going on and on,
And never really see me there.
I feel so invisible and no one really cares.
I try to do very well in school.
Sometimes I do and sometimes I don't
I get along with all my teachers
And am happy to see them every day.
I get along with some of my classmates,
but, some others don't really like me
My close friends are always there for me
I know that I usually overthink stuff
And probably this is all in my head.

The Seasons
by Charlotte King

Summertime in all its glory,
Fishing poles and fire-side stories.
Swimming pools and ice cream cones,
Trips to the beach and skipping stones.
Next comes Autumn, red and gold.
Raking leaves in the approaching cold.
Animals are sleeping, afraid of what's ahead.
The chilly bite of snow, and hiding in their bed.
The ends of the year, top and bottom.
Winter is coming, it's time for fun.
Hear the bells ringing, and the carolers singing.
Playing out in the snow, planning time for sledding.
The rainy season and blooming buds,
Planting flowers and digging in mud.
Spring is here and animals awake,
Bathing in the Sun's golden wake.
Those are the Seasons,
the times of the year.
Summer, Autumn,
Winter, and Spring!

Skyrim
by Elikem Amenuvor

Birch trees and wooded pines,
swaying in the forest,
Multicolored leaves and pine cones, lying on the ground,
Towering mountains, white as the clouds,
Geysers blasting scalding water and steam,
Gigantic six legged creatures with venomous fangs,
Humans as large as flagpoles swinging clubs,
Unsightly bandits travelling in gangs,
barbarians clad in animal hides,
Caves wrought with flames, arrows, and spikes,
Concealing their priceless treasures from the unworthy eye,
Sparks propelling from the palm of your hand,
Conjuring familiars drawn to your command,
Chairs and pots levitating in an inn,
Illuminating all that dares to be dark
Mystical forces with their encompassing shield,
Devastating dragons, stalking their prey,
burning, freezing, and electrified scales,
Slain, slaughtered, and bones left to rot,
Signs that with the Dragonborn they had fought.

Dare To Dream
by Zahava Klatzko

It's your wild imagination
To kids like us they teach
Your dreams, unrealistic
And are well beyond your reach
Yet sometimes when I'm all alone
Each star shines extra bright
I reach for one and swing from it
And dream with all my might
I dream up the impossible
I sprout my wings and fly
I climb the moon and dodge each star
and soar through heaven's sky
I find a world of love and light
Of kindness and of care
Where happiness is tangible
Something we all can share
For now, this dream is just a spark
But pray that in its time
It will shout my name and call for me
And I'll come and claim me mine

Title
by Jack Regino

Thinking and thinking and thinking away,
On what to write on this cold, rainy day.
The greatest ideas I can never seem to unmask,
Those ideas I need now, there's nothing more to ask.
Oh, I have a wonderful idea,
I will write about a rotting vessel and its drunken ransacking crew.
That's not bland but just untrue,
So that story won't do.
And now I'm once again stumped,
Looking at this screen, my shoulders slumped.
New ideas seem so accessible to other minds,
So how can mine be so blind?
Distractions are imminent,
Focus and be diligent.
Life is full of beautiful, colorful adventures,
I'll write about someone with many indentures.
No, that won't work,
New and refreshing ideas seem to lurk.
Right out of sight,
Oh, I know exactly what to write!

Daydreams
by Sarah Mlyn

The world around you swirls to dust
As you're whisked away to an alternate dreamland.
The world quickly fades to nothingness
And everything has come to a stop.
The constant movement
Of everything and everyone has finally slowed.
The moments are once again yours.
Ripped pages from books are once again restored
Along with the remnants of your shattered heart.
Everything is put back in its place.
But as quickly as it was built,
It comes crashing down.
The colors start to fade.
It's all gone, but never forgotten.
Unfairly ripped away
From your hopeless clutch.
The pages are once again torn.
Nothing but a sketch is left,
And you can't help but wish
What you had was real.

The Stalker
by Brady Crow

It creeps along the tattered wall,
Each slender leg climbing to torture the helpless.
Its beady eyes searching for something to devour,
Something new to add to the menu.
The monstrous fangs roar to awakening,
The glistening blades make your blood race,
Its foreboding, yet nimble, gait is well adapted for a chase,
Yet it doesn't have to.
Its home, an intricacy of silk and foolish leaves who ventured too close,
At a second's notice the beast is ready to pounce,
But the monster possesses patience,
Like a mouse in a trap, just waiting for its own demise.
Alas, a vulnerable target enters the web of trickery,
A nuisance, antsy to return home.
But its lack of self restraint proved to be its demise.
One wrong wing flap and it lands right into the killer's lair.
It flails, squirms, and rolls about, but exhaustion soon wins the fight.
The fearsome creature closes in on its prey as fast as a bolt of lightning.
In the game of life, only the strong survive,
That includes the ones with the strongest wills.

What Does Life Hold?
by Michelle Lawrence

What does life hold?
What does life hold?
Could it hold miracles?
Small ones and Big ones
The tiniest baby is born
Will it survive?
Every day a code blue is given
And nurses rush to the situation
Oxygen is pushed up through a tube
And heart rate is monitored
One day at last
There is a day to rejoice
The baby is home and doing just fine
What does life hold?
What does life hold?
Could it hold deaths?
A 93 year old is doing so well
But one day a tragic message goes out
A great-grandchild nothing but 1-year old
Doesn't remember Mamma Ann

Life On Earth
by Daniel Perrie

Seeping through the overgrowth
The Sun forever shines
The Moon assists with light reflected
Creeping through the vines
Vines creep forth spiraling
Reaching for the light
Stars dancing gracefully
Brightening the night
The Moon's companions
Stars of white
Not seen through day,
But seen through night
Earth's vast green jungle
Like the ocean
Never sleeping
In constant motion
Altogether these bring life
brought through pain and brought through strife
Yet in the end it shows its worth
Because that is life here down on Earth

2020 Rising Stars Collection

Bye Bye Bullying
by Nandini Krithivasan

Those people are normal.
They are no different than the rest.
Respect them just the same
It is for the best.
They just need a little help,
To do each and every task.
So keep on that kind smile,
And talk off that mean mask.
From no arm there,
To ADHD,
One should never be mean
About disabilities.
Say bye bye to bullying
Respect will always rise
One should never take in
Any of its nasty lies
Say bye bye to bullying
Why, throw it out the door.
One's good side should conquer
So not one will feel sore

Tolerance
by Taylor Peavy

Tolerance can be found almost anywhere,
You just need to look in the right places to find it.
But if you look in the wrong places it can feel hard to bear,
School shootings and drug abuse are wrong but seem hard to quit.
There are many problems we have in the world,
And the biggest are the ones we make.
Some people look toward Africans with fists curled,
Hands clenched so tightly you can see them quake.
How we view the world matters.
It is easy to see as a swirling black void,
With rumors, and lies filling chatter.
But listening, honesty and patience keeps us from being destroyed.
In communication, you may not agree,
Listening lets you hear what others are trying to say.
In this situation, honesty is key.
Patience isn't easy, but must be practiced every day.
While it seemed things got worse.
A generation will lead and change the world.
Through dialogue that is not coerced.
Tomorrow will always be better than the day before.

Cyberbullying
by Anisha Kodali

Social media is amusing,
Till one of the users starts blustering
The victims think their appearance is at fault
When really it is the bully's broken heart
Bullies think they are safe
Because they are hiding behind a screen that does not show their face
But if you have doubts because of a comment
Remember they only exist at that moment.
You look at your phone
And see something that makes you groan
someone decided to be pesky
And call you beastly
If you are sad
Because someone called you something bad
You should know
That they don't know how your personality glows
Don't put someone down
Even if you have a frown
Instead shine your flashlight brighter than the rest
Without being somebody else's pest

Human Being | Being Human
by Max Jose

Everyone should be born equal and free
With the ability to agree or disagree
Everyone should be given equal human rights
It's fundamental, not just a matter of being polite
Everyone is equal in the eyes of the law
Whether you are rich, or poor, an honoured citizen, or one with a flaw
We should be allowed to pray to any God we like
In the end they are all gods, they are all alike
We all have the right to life, liberty, and personal security
And should be treated as beings with respect and dignity
To live a life free from discrimination is our right
And we should not give it up without a fight
Everybody deserves freedom of thought and speech
That is what our teachers explain and preach
All of us deserve the right to education
As we all are a part of the future generation
As humans we all have the capacity to endure pain
Because without a struggle there is no gain
Being human and being treated as one is our most important right
And as human beings we should protect it with all of our might

Save Me From Fear
by Arianna Graziani

I woke up to the sound of devils,
they banged the door, it was dawn.
They were not dreams, they were not revels,
and all we have, it will now be gone.
Inside my mind I hear a voice,
I have many doubts, but I will go.
My dad will stay, we have no choice,
I need a place where I can grow.
With walk of pain, Rio Grande I see
I finally arrived at the bloody river,
I see my future, I want to break free.
The thunder struck, and I start to shiver.
In just an instant I was snatched,
on the dark ground, I have only tears.
We are many kids, and we are all scratched,
we are only numbers, plenty of fears.
We are not free, and here I'm too,
Will you help me, and let me in?
I may be different, but I am like you,
If we are friends, we all can win.

Today Is the Day
by Natalia Anderson

On our large Earth lies the astonishing ocean.
It creates a graceful-moving motion.
Sadly, it is slowly rotting away.
Its color tarnishing and turning into a dark gray.
Today is the day where my Earth will be better.
The ocean will shine crystal clear.
Uncontaminated water that people can be near.
The ocean will give off better air
And in return, the humans will treat it fair.
Today is the day where my Earth will be better.
The turtles stuck in large masses of sickening plastic wrap will be set free.
And all the seals and their fuzzy pups will be filled with glee.
The whales can continue to create their beautiful sounds
And we'll all come together to clean up the plastic mounds.
Today is the day where my Earth will be better
This horrible situation cannot stay silent
Because the revolting trash in the ocean has become violent.
I cannot let these harmful pieces of trash invade.
I cannot let our strong and vast animal population fade.
Today is the day where my Earth will be better.

Math
by Nora Mayne

Fractions, decimals, percentages too,
Don't know about you but I have no clue
Whether to add, multiply or even reduce,
Math to me is just mental abuse
Geometry, algebra, and there's even more,
Math is no better even with common core
All the mental math and no writing things down,
I think I might have a mental breakdown
Angles, graphs, and integers too,
Now I even wonder if I will pull through
Reciprocals for me are confusing enough,
Why do people make us learn this stuff
Triangles, circles and squares, oh my,
What is the point, I won't even try
The talk of math makes me so stressed,
Math will never meet my interest
Addends, subtrahends, minuends too,
I wonder if I'll ever pull through
We're not allowed to use calculators,
Math in my life is like one giant crater.

This New World
by Alexander Polyansky

In a world that was once anew,
in a place where the sky was blue.
The hands of man tore it down,
until nothing was left on ground.
The vines of greed crept up the walls.
The molds of need defaced the halls.
The flies of hatred flew aloof.
The crows of power topped the roof.
As we tore Mother Nature down,
no matter how much God would frown.
The line of man, the length was long.
In the history of all we did wrong.
The wars, the pain,
This was all part of our terrible reign
As Mother Nature cowered in fear,
nothing we did was very clear.
But when we are gone and put to rest,
Mother Nature will be at her best.
In a place where the sky was blue
In a world that was once anew.

Years of Our Life
by Elizabeth Paskey

The times were carefree
Just you and me
Then the little ones
The long sleepless nights
Then they were walking
Next the school supplies
The sports, the friendship, and the fun
They were getting older
and we were growing wise
Then the bump on the log stage
The mood and acne
Also more responsibilities
It all seemed to disappear
One went away, the other followed too
Off to their studies
Leaving us behind
They found their partners
Our new names came too
We are getting older
and they are growing wise

The Grumpy Stranger In New York City
by Riyan Mehta

One day at a pet shop,
I met a man selling puppies,
For money he wanted to swap,
But I really wanted some guppies.
"Got any guppies?" asked I.
"For that's how I'll spend my money."
"No guppies here!" said the guy.
He seemed to find it quite funny.
"We've got some lovely kittens,
I'll give you a very fine price."
"I'd rather have some mittens."
The man blinked rapidly thrice.
The man seemed exceptionally mean,
And his manner was strangely amused.
He wasn't what I would call treen,
Great disdain he noticeably oozed.
Like others, he thought I was odd,
Some say I'm a bit grumpy.
Still he gave me a courteous nod,
As if he thought I was plenty scrimpy.

A Memory
by Kristin Ackerman

There is a snowflake that falls
like a distant dream
We try and try
to make it land on our noses,
but it rarely does.
It falls for miles
into a parallel universe-
joining the rest below.
A memory
we try to remember
but just can't.
Now we miss the lonely memories
that have fallen like snowflakes
and melted away,
lost with so many others.
Let me tell you this-
when it falls, on a cold winter day,
catch that snowflake.
Don't let it disappear.

Train Ride
by Claudia Idioma

This train I'm riding
It's moving too fast
I don't want to move forward
I want to go back to the past.
I don't want to see people depart this train
My family, my friends, my cherished ones
Just thinking about it gives me pain
I'm afraid of what the future will hold
Please, tell me, why do I have to grow old?
Hasn't the train ride just begun?
I'm dreading what will happen when it's done.
The speed is unbearable
Where has my youth gone?
I wish this were Minecraft so I could respawn.
Life is a train that we all have boarded
It may seem too fast or too slow at times but just know,
That you should live every moment,
Enjoy each second,
So you won't think of this train ride as your foe.

The Robin Eggs
by Madalyn Benson

The blue robin eggs
The robin eggs were little
The robins were cute

The Last Shot
by Alinur Najim

One more minute on the clock
All I hear is tick tock
Passing and dribbling back and forth
Thinking of how much the last shot is worth
Holding the ball in my hand
I take a breath and mark my stand
I prepare myself to make the shot
And make sure to give it all I got
I shoot the ball
I shoot it right
Now is the time to end this fight.

The Junkyard of Memories
by Claire Terhune

Darkness comes over me like a glove.
Eyes bright red, and mind cleared.
A bright, white light then cuts through me like a boomerang
coming back to its owner.
Fallen. Regret. Forgotten just like this big, old junkyard of memories.
Mistakes made ... One after another!
Junk. All junk.
Lay. Eyes open.
I try and tell myself for I want to live again, but my pain will not bend.
So I sat, as I watched the years grow wings and fly away to my junkyard.
The junkyard of broken dreams, where I found my savior, but lost my hope.
The same junkyard where I fall into prying arms of fate and destiny.
Should I let the person in the mirror take control?
Am I nothing but the down of everybody else's up?
I will be STRONG, I will be BRAVE, I will be ME.
Get up. All I can see is bright light, coming from every direction;
reaching out to touch my pale face.
I might fall or trip, but I will get up anyway.
I feel frozen in space, arms and legs tightly placed to my sides-
But, I let the sun in - RUN, RUN, RUN in the burning sun!

Smart
by Haley DiFilippo

Am I smart
I don't think so
But I will never really know
What makes us smart
Is it the tests they give
Or the life we live
If I am not smart
How can I ever be
I wonder if I will ever see
What makes us smart
I guess we will never know
What makes us so

You're Fine!
by Amira Ismail

- While I gasp for air, you say breathe
- While I fidget, you say calm down
- I'm dying, is this ever going to end?
- Overthinking, overlooking, overreacting, you say
- Chest heavy, heart racing 800 MPH
- Overdramatic, she doesn't have a reason you say
- What are they thinking?
- Cold sweats rushing in
- Is this a panic attack?
- Am I dying? Is someone going to help?
- You're fine, it's just fear, you say

Life Will Always Be a Question
by Norah Frank

Every day I spend waiting
Because it feels like time is fading
If I chase the stars, will I fall?
Why do all my dreams seem too tall?
I just want to be happy again
I wish I had more friends.
I wish I could go to bed.
Why does life always seem so baiting?
Why are all of my interests decaying?
Why do I always feel at fault?
I guess that's just how life works.
I guess we all have our quirks.

Rushing Spring
by Elsa Menter Jones

Tender
Slowly opening
Like a flower after the first gentle rains
A smile where a frown was
Hands lingering for a second longer
A soft gaze
Wishing to unfold you and see all your sides
Touch
Quick, hurry
We might get shot up
The world is melting
Trash is suffocating
Help!
But how can we?
Work harder
It's never enough
We'd need to be really great
That could never be us
We can start with love

Stress
by Alexandra Radinsky

Stress comes down like rain
You can get shelter.
But until you pull out the umbrella
You will get soaked.
Sometimes we don't pull out the brolly, and get drenched
The rain doesn't stop
As it drippity drops.
Down, down, down
Drip, drop.
A new worry, and then the anxiety rolls in like thunder.
CRASH!
So many thoughts, and getting so wet.
Before you know it there's a storm.
Panic. Panic everywhere,
But up there
In your head it won't stop.
The sun will come out eventually.
Just wait.
Drip, drop, crash, drip, drip, and silence.

I Fall
by Rebekah Setti

I start to crawl then I fall,
I start to walk then I fall,
I start to ride my bicycle then I fall,
I start to balance then I fall,
I start to dance then I fall,
I start to flip then I fall,
I start to run then I fall,
I start to dribble then I fall,
I start to kick then I fall,
I start to pitch then I fall,
I start to catch then I fall,
I start to read then my attention falls,
I start to build then it falls,
I start to act then I fall,
I start to draw then the pencil falls,
I start to live life then I fall,
I may always fall,
But I will never stay down.

Where I'm From
by Miley Contreras

I am from my restaurant-owning sister
my hard-working electrician dad
from my restaurant-owning sister
to my world-travelling brother
from my funny *Fortnite* brother
and my always working mom
I am from my favorite Peruvian restaurant
Chocolate sundae Sundays
Dad's delicious seviche Saturdays
I am from listening to inspiring music
drawing 'til dawn with my brother
"Crash," from learning to ride a bike
I am from eating chips on trips to Pennsylvania, New York, and Florida
"Boom!" to seeing the fireworks in the bright night sky at the Magic Kingdom.
I am from getting shiny silver staples in my head
from winning National Champions
to Runners-Up at Globals for cheer
"Snip, snip," being aware of donating my hair
Most of all, having no tears, no fears
I am Miley Contreras

Winter Wonderland
by Alexa Collins

Remember those bitter days?
The fireplace ablaze.
Riding on Santa themed sleighs.
Watching Christmas ballets.
Singing along to Christmas carols.
Giving good to those 'round barrels
or roasting on the fire, an array of arils.
Sitting 'round the fire,
Children practicing for church choir.
The cookies in the oven rising higher.
Revisiting tradition's abandoned prior.

Life
by Moriah Ince

You can have choices
You can choose to fight or surrender
You can choose to love or lose
You can choose to be mean or kind
You can choose to cry or not
You can choose to make enemies or friends
You can choose to talk or stay mute
You can choose to scream aloud or in your head
You have the choice, life is full of choices
Choose wisely!
I choose to live my best life, because life is short and every day is a struggle

The Island of Compromise
by Mason Scherer

After many fateful days
A symbol of freedom and liberty
Was raised above an island
Ridden with bodies that were fighting between democracy and imperialism
And after the battle
Four brave souls, of American origin
Raised the American flag
On what was an island controlled by fascists
Now in Allied hands
Although the loss was tragic
It would soon conclude World War II

Swift
by Malcolm Ureña

Moving, proceeding
Or acting with
Great speed
As in I move
Swift when in practice
I'm gliding across the rink
When I shoot it's like a shooting star
The winning goal
I'm not even trying
It's like I'm swimming in a pool of clouds
The game 7-3

Reading At Midnight
by Sophie Stetts

I stepped into my own world,
the fluttering of a new page,
my stomach curled,
with the heartache of age.
Pushing through,
until the bells of midnight ring,
in just a moment I'll break through,
I have no idea what the next page will bring.
This is better than any world before,
this is the last page,
just one more.

Anger
by Mia Sara Torres

Anger tastes like a Carolina reaper pepper, nasty and hot.
You think you can take the spice but when people leave you run to let it out.
Anger feels like loneliness with no one to talk to.
Anger feels like you not spitting out that spicy pepper in front of people
to express the pain you are going through.
Anger smells like garbage everyone inhales the smell.
But ... anger actually smells like the air freshener that demolishes the smell.
Anger is you spitting out that pepper and telling people about the pain you felt.
Anger is loneliness but then someone comes.
Anger is you not eating the pepper in the first place.

For the Better
by Katharine Sheahan

She left for better
My heart clenches this sadness
She is happier
It is for the best
The second time she has gone
This time was for good
Her life here was bad
Her life now is blossoming
I miss her dearly
She is my best friend
She is a piece in my heart
Try to stitch the wound
Most people forget
Not bothered by her absence
But she brings me bliss
She may be gone
But in the light I see her
My bestie always.

Halloween Ball
by Roselynn Fredericksdorf

Halloween night was afright.
I already hear the ghosts howl,
and the werewolves start to prowl.
Zombies wake up all grumpy and mad,
while skeletons dance all happy and proud.
Spirits fly to the moon and back,
pumpkins come alive and hide behind your back.
Spooky and scary stories are told,
ones about you getting put in a hole.
Bats fly over your head making weird noises,
then you start to hear scary voices.
If you feel scared, they don't care.
If you feel happy, they'll make you feel sappy.
There's not just ghosts, werewolves, zombies.
There's talking dummies, bigfoot, and yetis.
"Are you scared yet?" I ask.
You say, "No, not at all."
Then I'll have to try harder next year at the Halloween ball.

From Forests to Plains
by Nicholas Del Buono

From forests to plains.
Where it's sunny and where it rains.
Places around the world we see.
Life flourishes and runs free.
From fire and floods
To hurricanes
Throughout the rubble
Life still reigns
Rainforests so big and lush
Up in the trees
Inside the brush
In the sky it rains all day
And all of the birds fly away
Snakes slither all around
They go in their dens beneath the ground.
Throughout the plains in the dark.
You can see a tiny spark of the beautiful world to see.
Which is wonderful for you and me.

Where I'm From
by Haley Frushon

I'm from watching football in the fall.
From doing leaps around my house.
I'm from dancing in the blue room with the marly floor in it.
I'm from Emotion in Motion Dance Center.
I'm from planting flowers with my nana and poppy on Mother's Day.
From making cakes and pies with them too.
I'm from Nana's best home-cooked dinners in town.
I'm from Mom, Dad, Nana, and Papa.
From Sandy, Wednesday, Missie, and Peanut.
From Alana and Uncle Tony.
I'm from seeing hippos for the first time at the zoo.
I'm from riding my favorite roller coaster, Mount Everest.
I'm from the splashing sound in the pool.
I'm from singing in the backyard in the summer.
I'm from my mom's amazing meatballs.
From my nana's cheerful chicken cutlets.
I'm from my dad's bacon cheeseburgers on warm summer nights.
I am Haley Frushon

Till Death Do Us Part
by Zoai Ehrgott

The days got longer.
Is my heart stronger?
When can I live?
All I do is give.
When can I take?
Why does my heart still ache?
Till death do us part,
That's what they all say.
But mom broke dad's heart,
Its dying each day.
He feels so alone.
Mom doesn't stay home.
I'm trying to stay strong,
But why is this taking so long?
Till death do us part
It's such a fake lie,
Because mom broke dad's heart,
And he didn't even die.

Where I'm From
by Ava Jansen

I am from sparkling rhinestones on my green uniform,
From watching the Yankees games.
And watching the football games at Gianna's school.
I am from drinking a sweet strawberry milkshake from Carvel,
To perfect grilled cheese sandwiches made by Dad,
And Frappuccinos from Starbucks.
I'm from a magnificent mom,
A good-humored dad,
A cute, loving dog named Benley,
And a glamorous sister, Gianna, a Livoti's cashier.
I am from the last memories I had with a family member,
From dallying around on the computer playing *Purble Place* with Uncle Bob,
To playing the clarinet, just like Uncle Mike.
I'm from helping Nanny watch Livvy,
From going to the mall for special occasions,
And going out to dinner with Nanny and Poppy whenever Mom and Dad went out.
I'm from Christmas Eve parties at Aunt Angie's house,
From the boom of fireworks on the Fourth of July,
To the loud noises at Thanksgiving feasts.
I am Ava Jansen

Bear Care
by Leona Beiler

There once was a bear
who had only one hair
and he sat in my chair
And I started to stare.
Then he went to the kitchen
and started eating my chicken
and drinking my water, oh bother.
And when he was full of chicken and things
he went to my bird and plucked out its wings.
Then I got mad
and sent him to dad
And dad set him straight
and gave him to me. again.
So I took him to school
but you know it's the rule
no pets in a school.
So I was stuck with that bear
who had only one hair.

Current Events
by Anna Rossman

Every week a current event is due.
But nothing good comes from the news.
They sing a sweet sad song of blues.
Blood and violence leap from the pages
Like ghostly echoes bouncing off empty cages.
I sit and read as the world around me rages.
Dreams destroyed into dust
Iron doors of opportunity reduced to rust
They all fall to greed and lust.
Everyone wants the illustrious crown
Until they dare to glance down
At their own cynical chaos crumbling the town.
The crown's now a burden they must bear
While death deftly takes his hefty share.
I read about it in current events everywhere.
I wish there was more I could do
To stop the ringing of the sweet sad tune.
Still nothing good comes from the news.

Woods
by Olivia Crum

The woods are spooky
in the night you hear roaring
Beware of the woods

Dirt Bikes
by Giovanni Kruppa

Dirty all the time
I ride in my field
Race my friends
Try to do fender scrapes

Beat everyone in races
I ride every day
Keep control of the bike
Excellent riding skills
Splashing through mud!

Life
by Lily Grant

Angelically beautiful
Beaming with individuality
Creatively yours
Dazzling to the eyes yet not always to the mind
Elegantly pleasing
Faithful if you make it
Gracefully perfect
Heart-stopping disasters
Illogical at times
Jinxed some may say
Keen for action
Lyrically made, but
Magically distant
Native to you
Opulent with love
Passion filled
Quondam seemingly perfect
Rustic at heart
Secure, stable yet not forever
Temporary
Undeserving of praise
Virtually controlled
Weathered vitality
Xenial
Yonder to the end
Zippy

Cats
by Eliyah Czebiniak

Cats are awesome, cats are cute
But they cannot play the flute
They play and run, catch mice all day
No cats are blue, but some are gray
Their babies are so very cute
Their babies are called kittens
The fur God gave them is so warm
That they do not need mittens
I love cats, girl or boy
When I see them, it brings me joy
Luna was my favorite cat
I think I ever had
Every time I saw him
He always made me glad.

The Cycle of the Sky
by Leisa Mitchell

The sun is shining very bright
Eventually it turns to night
The bright stars then take its place
As if they were trying to win a race.
The stars are gleaming in the night sky,
Looking down on us.
We sleep under their bright light
While they twinkle at us all night.
The stars slowly start to fade away
For the sun is rising up our way
We can still see their light
It's just not as bright.
The sun finally rises in the sky
Now I have to say goodbye.

Rain
by Alivia Herzog

The rain falls down in small drops,
each one unique in its own way.
R in rain, as in rise from and stand tall.
A, as in accomplish something that you are proud of, not disappointed in;
make it something that's worth accomplishing.
I, as in independence; be an example to yourself
and be a part of someone else's example too.
Lastly, **N**, as in noble and having good moral standards
and knowing when to speak and when not to speak
by considering people's feelings.
Rain, a unique word that can describe unique people.

Tears of Blue
by Sara Praszkowicz

Tears come and go.
But when they come they remind you
Of pain and the past.
Whether you're happy or blue.
Tears express our feelings.
Tears let go of our feelings
even when you might not want to.

Halloween
by Jonathan Ward

Happy Halloween
I said to the queen
I like your skeleton bones
Around your phone.
I watched your black cat
Hunt a black rat
And that was the end of that.

Stay
by Marty Widmer

Here I lay
In my bed
Wanting to slay
The demons in my head
Their eyes bright red
They say no fun
I need to shun
The demons in my head
They need to be released
So I can lay in peace
But even through my snoring
All I hear is them roaring
With the demons screaming
All I want is to be dreaming
But all I do is wonder
If the demons in my head will get slaughtered
Why are there demons
There is no reason
Every season
There is no reason
They are here to stay
And I cannot slay
So, welcome home demons
You're welcome to stay

Basketball
by Joseph Grimaldi

Dribbling, shooting, passing
All the things to win the game
I dribble across the court
I shoot from half court
I pass the ball to the point guard
Dribbling, shooting, passing
All the things to win the game

A Star
by Ireisha Patton

A star is a heart that flows in the dark.
Traversing the electric sky.
Love is a desire to set us apart.
We exist in the blink of an eye.
One day we will all go back to one to remember who it is we are.
All the hearts falling back home to the sun, the reflections of a star.
When I get older I will become a peaceful star.

I Didn't Think I Could Write This Poem
by Kate Petri

I didn't think I could write this poem,
I didn't want to try.
I didn't think any ideas would come to me,
I didn't think they'd amount to anything.
That's what I thought at first.
Why was I so negative?
There's so much negativity in the world.
I didn't, I don't, I can't, I won't,
That's what everyone says.
Why can't we be more positive?
I did, I do, I can, I will,
That's what everyone should say.
If we all changed our viewpoints,
If we gave encouraging thoughts,
If we spread positivity,
The world would be a better place.
I did write this poem,
I bothered to try.
Ideas came to me,
And they amounted to something.
I didn't think I could write this poem,
But I changed my viewpoint,
And now, I have a whole world of possibilities,
Right here in front of me.

Makeup Smears
by Corbi McGovern

Makeup smears
Bruises heal
Tears dry
Pain fades
Memories last
Tears return
Pain arrives
Anxiety forms
Sadness grows
Memories vanish
Love enters
Anxiety disappears
Sadness hides
Smiles form
Voices raise
Someone leaves
Sadness appears
Anxiety crawls back
Smiles fade
Tears fall

Now read it backwards

You Are Not Alone
by Jasmin Mendes

The rain runs down my face.
I smile and wipe my tears,
And whisper, I have to stay strong.
Even though I feel alone, like no one cares.
I felt empty and invisible.
But then a group of girls came and gave me the biggest hug.
It turns out they all saw me get bullied
And couldn't believe that happened.
I said I was ok but they all knew I wasn't.
We said goodbye and went home.
The next day I was getting bullied
But this time I didn't cry, I smiled
'Cause I opened my eyes to see the same group of girls,
standing in front of me yelling at the bullies
They helped me up and I hugged them
I say thank you and they said that's what we do for our friends.
That's when I realized
I'm never alone.

The Vicious Truth
by Annabella Chaklos

Every single day, they watch us like a hawk.
We were given voices, but we aren't allowed to talk.
All of us are placed into one, long, straight line.
We all must be perfect, not good, not fine.
It's now getting foggy, and thoughts are ceasing.
Why are all the dreams and creativity decreasing?
However they can yell, and say it's all because of the way we act.
They are just upset because of the well known fact.
I no longer have memories to reminisce.
I'm being taken into a quiet, mindless bliss.
Our imaginations are soon to disintegrate.
This is all that is left, this our fate.
The youth of this generation is being terminated.
Brainless creatures are being created.
Smiles and laughs turn into stone and silence.
Why is this, just because of a little defiance?
You believe we are evil, with no intelligence or love.
Do you not remember what your youth consisted of?

Where I'm From
by Christopher Everett

I am from scoring the game-winning point
I am from getting 2 hat tricks in a single game
To jumping straight into waves with my brothers
From the best juke I've ever done.
I am from getting amazing teachers
and friends who make me laugh
From a hard-working mom
and playing with friends and having great times
I'm from watching SpongeBob and Tom and Jerry as I was growing up
To having a roof over my head
And my brother blasting his music
To getting my very first phone
I am from unfinished pool parties
To banging pots at New Year's Eve
I am from Pop's famous chili
To Grandma's famous potatoes and egg
I'm from having pizza night with Pop and Grandma
I am from crazy loud roller coasters
To being hilarious.
Christopher Everett

El Paso
by Sofia Edlund

Not a breath more
Don't stress, no more.
Not a word more,
No longer heard more.
Please not again, Lord.
Now it's happening in stores.
Please don't hurt others;
We are all sisters and brothers.
Shoot, shoot, shoot no more.
I will not shoot for sure.
- This poem is dedicated to those
who lost their lives in the El Paso shooting.

The Way Things Used To Be
by Kearstin YounKin

I look around the world today
All I see is gray
What happened to the world my grandma talks about
I guess I'll never know
I guess I'll never see
The word my grandma talks about
She said of a time when the air was pure
And when the earth was clean
She said when she was young
People watched their tongue
I wonder what happened to the world my grandma talks about
Grandma said she is afraid of how the earth is turning
She said that there was peace
Which is now replaced with violence and chaos
She talks about a time when not everything was a race to be the most powerful
She said it was our fault
And that we can fix it
One bottle at a time
She said we would have to recycle
And ride our bicycles
My grandma doesn't say no more
I'm sad she had to go
Swallowed up by the world that made her sad
If I had one wish
I wish to see
To see the world my grandma talked about

The Invisible Helper
by Conleth Gorham

Although we might not realize,
The air is helping us in the skies.
However, the air today is badly affected,
But our polluting ways can be corrected.
The air supplies us with oxygen to inhale.
This is very important on a large-scale.
We are not the only ones benefiting from air,
If plants and animals did not have it, it would be a nightmare.
But today the air suffers from pollution
So for this problem we need a solution.
As normal people we could ride our bikes,
Or instead of driving take some hikes.
We could try to prevent smoking
Because on the smoke birds are choking.
We could plant more trees
We could do a lot of things that are easy and free.

Where I'm From
by Nicholas Gallo

I am from piles of diamond in *Minecraft*,
From *Fortnite Victory Royales*.
I am from video games online with friends,
From shopping at GameStop.
I'm from a mom with a desk job,
from a dad, a painter.
I am from a Barbie lovin' sister,
from myself, a video game freak.
From comparing candy on Halloween night.
I'm from brownies for dessert.
I'm from hot wings with no cooldown sauce,
from platters of fruit.
I am from travelling to Tennessee.
I'm from flying to Florida,
to camping in New York.
From four-square at recess,
from the school's questionable lunch.
I'm from straight A's,
from many tests and quizzes.
I am Nick Gallo

You Aren't Here
by Allyssa Turcot

I sit here alone,
Wondering why it's so cold.
Grabbing a hand,
That's not here anymore.
You're the ghost of the past,
But the past I can't let go of.
I cry deep inside,
Not understanding why.
You were the reason I live,
But now that excuse is gone.
You left me alone,
What did I do wrong?

Magic
by Karina Pedroza

I heard a mystical, crisp mesmerizing sound
No doubt that it was magic
It was temporizing, bloodcurdling, surprising!
And the exquisite notion ever entrancing
While I pondered, fascinated and a bit scared
My glory, I could not awaken
The silky sheen mesmerizing
Of the sun that is shining
Much I marveled this heartening magic.
The bewildering beauty bewitching
'It's that exuberance,' I muttered
Back into my memories thrilling
The amazing allure arousing
Magic is not real, you say?
That is not true, that is not true
For magic is not frolicking unicorns in lush fields
Princes and princesses, kings and queens
It is you
Anything that makes you happy, anything that is good
Magic is in the eye of the beholder

A Walk On the Beach
by Niki Feiner

Whose Beach is this, I think I might know
His Beach house is A Couple miles to go
He won't see me after hours
To watch the sun set below
Between the sand and ocean tides
The most beautiful place on Earth lies
The ocean waves sway side to side
While the sunset sets below the ocean tides

Believe To Succeed
by Samaya Khanali

You give me An inch,
I will take a mile
to succeed in my journey,
which may take a while,
for I am Driven,
this you will see,
a Creature From heaven,
Born to succeed.
As Far as I can remember,
my failures gave me strength,
I am truly determined to persevere at great length.
My family is my guidance,
my muse to the future,
without them I would Be lost,
no path to venture.
One must Embrace all the world has to give,
recognizing its value,
there are many reasons to live.
My inner strength existed since birth I've been told,
the history I am creating will soon unfold.
I will make strides and show those who don't believe
that I am quite the persistent being, I will achieve.
Believe in yourself and you will see
a future worth living and a life worth more than a dream.

A Real Queen
by Aaliah Ahmad

A real queen Doesn't need Fame,
A Crown, Fancy jewelry and clothes,
makeup or the power to rule other people's lives.
A real queen has the power to rule her own life,
she loves herself for who she is on the inside
and uses her head and her heart.

Live Life
by Sukhpreet Kaur

Living life is really great,
It's where you can participate.
Living life is so much fun,
the biggest challenges are to be done.
Living life is to thrive,
It's where you can be alive.
Living life is to be free
It is the key to love and sing!
It's time to end my poem now.
I depend on you to trust me ... Somehow!

The Changes of Life
by Luke Bowers

A day is a life
A life is a day
As dawn turns into the Break of day
Day turns into dusk
Flowers bloom
There is no gloom
Bees Flutter in the air
While bears are around Everywhere
As the leaves begin to change
The air becomes weaker with every breath
Snowflakes fall from the sky
With frost on the moss
And snowmen all through my mind
The seasons change before our eyes
As every day is unique in itself

When
by Clarissa Kuhn

When the light is off, turn it on.
When the day is cold, bring it warmth.
When the sky is dark, bring it color.
When someone is hurt, help them heal.
When someone starts crying, wipe the tears away.
When bubbles start popping, make more.
When someone needs help, be there.
When someone needs comfort, be there.
Then when you need something, people will be there for you.

Sadness
by Natalie Bellush

It's like you're surrounded by water
Getting pulled down into the darkness you can't escape
It's like anger, but with anger you have the fire to stay
and fight but with this you have no flame
It's like fear, but with fear comes the energy
To run, to scream, but with this you have none
It is not anger, not fear, not confusion, not worry
It's just sadness, that soft blanket
That covers your thoughts, blocking out the hope

Literate
by Tyler Butterfield

Reading helps me every day
To ease the tasks that are at bay.
I read short, long, easy and hard books.
Many of them give information
On our own very nation.
History, Adventures, Biographies will do
Journals, Articles, Newspapers too.
Reading is a good way to pass time
At a library it may only cost a dime!
Some books are available online.
I read them every single day
It will help me with my schoolwork today.

The Garden of Manhattan
by Chaya Willner

In the busiest city
That is my home
Of apartments pushed together
With no space of your own
It's much too crowded
For a breath of fresh air
And it's much to busy
For a kind word to spare
Yet in the busiest city
With no crowding solution
I have my very own garden
With not an ounce of pollution
When I'm alone
I can sit there for hours
It's ten acres long
And has hundreds of flowers
Common ones like roses
Or an edelweiss that's rare
Both types brought up by me
From infancy with care
To help my flowers grow
I have the perfect recipe
One half is water, the other sun
So they develop beautifully
Every color's perfect
White, green, pink, and blue
Purple, yellow, and peach
Each petal a different hue
And maybe you're wondering how
In Manhattan there's such a creation
I'll tell you the simple truth
It's my imagination
But in a city where there's no grass
And for a garden there's no space
And a town with too much people
Imagination will take its place

1ST PLACE

The Lie
by Emma Easter

Liberty isn't like it was before.
Independence has become forced.
Justice has migrated
From the side of the people
To the side of the press.
Falsities buzz around like flies to roadkill
Even if you can't see them quite yet.
They may not be clear to the eye,
But ever omniscient, they are always there.
Hovering above,
Floating just out of reach.
Gyrating like vultures over a battlefield
quietly, quietly.
Without a word, they descend,
Swallowing the Earth whole and us along with it.
And yet, we still believe them,
the ones sabotaging our world.
For they offer us what human beings cannot.
The life within a life.
The lie within us all.

DIVISION III

GRADES 9-12

The Days In Between the Seasons
by Madalynn Hill

Winter cracks in her skin,
Summer mourning in her eyes.
like apricot trees,
life will come sooner than you think.
Spring can hold my hand,
lead me to the collapse.
Autumn will sing
how he misses my delicate hands in the palm of his,
the fact they're good at loving.
and how much I can't feel the pain,
like the days we forget about.
the days in between the seasons.

I Hope I'll See You Again
by Natalie Barrows

Another day not spent with you
My heart doesn't know what to do
Time will pass and I may heal
But it won't change how I feel
Memories flashback inside of me
They can't hide, they just remind me
Of my one and only love
Moving on is harder than you could imagine
Everything I see reminds me of who we used to be
You were so much more than a friend
You were my everything until the end
I just gotta hope I'll see you again
Days may pass and years will come
You'll always be the one I dream of
You made me smile and made me cry
It's easy to see why I have a whole inside
Moving on is harder than you could imagine
Everything I see reminds me of who we used to be
You were so much more than a friend
You were my everything until the end
I just gotta hope I'll see you again
I can't dwell on the past
Things have started to change real fast
I'm not who I was ever since you had to leave me
But I will always honor your memory
Moving on is harder than you could imagine
Everything I see reminds me of who we used to be
You were so much more than a friend
You were my everything until the end
I just gotta hope I'll see you again
I just gotta hope I'll see you again

Honest
by Channing Prins

I always wonder, I never ask
I sometimes type everything up,
And leave the backspace for last.
I do not ask, I don't want to cause pain.
I leave my questions to my wondering brain.
I don't want to hurt you. So I don't ask
My questions are my mind's task.
As I fall asleep each night, I think of you,
And I wonder if you have questions too.
I will wait for you, until you send me a sign,
Then maybe I'll ask. And hope I don't cross the line.
So that one day when I ask, please promise
That you won't hate me for being honest.

The Color of My Skin
by Ariana Rivera

Why must the color of my skin be like a cage
Something that holds me back from ever amounting to anything
Something that prevents me from achieving anything
Why must it dictate so much, my education, my career, the college I attend
All dictated by something so simple. Why must it matter
I was always told to be proud of my heritage
Yet how can I do this when my heritage is being discriminated against
How can I be proud of something that makes me lower than the rest
Why must my gender make me less valid than you
A social injustice that I thought we put an end to fifty years ago
But I get it, the whole double negative thing
I'm a Puerto Rican young woman
And that somehow makes me less of a person
Even though I was told we're all equal
Why am I a statistic, a number on a chart
Because if where I go to school has a reputation
of having uneducated people of color
Somehow I become one of them, because obviously we're all the same
I have a name you know
Why am I still fighting a war that I thought was already won
When we decided that men and women were equal
I guess they forgot to mention that people of color were left out of that equation
Why must I have to break a glass ceiling to have my name recognized
In a world of people who just don't pay attention
Why, I don't understand, someone enlighten me
And if not, let me get this through your heads
I am not a number, another statistic on a chart, another stereotype
I am proud to say I'm an intelligent, creative, Puerto Rican girl
Who plans to make a difference, and when I do
You best believe you'll know my name

The Power of Light
by Courtney Thompson

With faith beneath her
She let her true self shine
The old version of who she was faded away
Without hesitation she began to be herself
Never once stepping back into the darkness she once hid in
Light filled the space around her
Lighting up the darkest of places around her
When she awoke every morning
She never once let her smile falter
Whatever the day brought
She faced it with a smile and the confidence within
Letting the light from inside shine
The darkness of the world was destroyed around her

If Satan Was a Black Boy
by Ethan Olidge-Evans

It's funny to me
How God chose a black boy to rule his underworld
A testament
To how death can turn slaves into kings
To how black boys only find life in death
Find purpose in their demise
See most people go to Church
But the streets have always been my place of worship
It is there that I pray
Two hands up
Before my badged savior baptizes me with bullets
My body riddled with crimson Halos
At least in death I am Holy
I like to consider myself a Prophet after all
Is the gunshot not their Word of God
A sign of His divine intervention
Which goes to show
That they see no difference between
A hoodie and horns
So I become the monster they want me to be
My hands of divinity bare clenched fist
You've killed so many of us
You could mistake our numbers for mutiny
A revolution that transcends life itself
This is retaliation
I will give birth to movements
I will burn your privilege to ashes
My name isn't Trayvon Martin anymore
It's not Tamir Rice
I am Satan

Body Count
by Alyssa Grasso

One two three four
The media's words smooth like purrs
Five six seven eight
A demonic horde our lives as bait
Nine ten eleven twelve
Broken rosaries adored shattered shelves
Thirteen fourteen fifteen sixteen
Bodies laid out, bloody and green
Seventeen eighteen nineteen twenty
The children lean forward,
"And then? And then?"
Blood falls and bones break
After all this time
bombed children won't wake

Turquoise - 9/21/19
by Alex McCune

Finding out you never cared about me
it's like I always knew and forgot to tell myself
You made me feel special and different but I was like all the rest you
found and left crumpled up like scrap paper
tossed in the bin you lit on fire that summer
When we first met you were like a breath of fresh air
and I got used to breathing you
Each breath was burning my lungs
but I was so used to the pain that when it stopped it hurt
I never really decided to leave you and I still don't think I have
Your toothbrush is still by my sink and your pillow on my bed
still smells like the alcohol we spilled on it that day you lit your hand on fire
I will always remember the time you took me to the beach in Malibu
and you watched me surf from the shore
because you never learned how to swim
I always said I'd teach you but we never had the time
You taught me some wonderful things
and I've found that since you're gone it's hard to do them the way I used to
I will never forget how you would hold me at night
and we would smile and laugh and forget about time
until the morning sun would shine through my window
You gave me your hand when I was scared to cross the river
on the tree that fell down when it was super windy that one day
and helped me forget my fears
I always said I'd never let you go and you said the same to me
so why did you leave
You haven't sent me a letter in a really long time
so I'm stuck reading all the old ones
So please come back before my lungs get used to the air again.

Write Me Something Pretty
by Costello Keene

Lovely rosebushes with pink petals speckled with dew
Gold leaf pasted to walls of cherubs lined a golden room
Tall handsome pine trees set neatly in a line
Red and white ornaments wrapped 'round its branches with twine
Hot steam and rich potatoes, melting in your mouth
The warm breeze and bits of sand blowing from the south
Hands as soft as butter, even fleece or maybe silk
Kitchens during midnight hosting cookies dipped in milk
Warm wooly mittens, wrapped around small fingers
And scents of chocolate oranges always seem to linger
Tea in fancy teacups, rich black and brown and green
Kittens with tiny tongues licking their orange fur clean
Write me something pretty, she said with a smile
And so I sat and wrote, typing for quite a while

The Living
by Haize Camacho

You,
You are the brave and fearless
The courage and power
The hope of many
In which they wish to devour
You are a soldier
You are not a coward
Because of all the dirt you are the only flower
You,
You strike fear in your enemies,
show tremendous strength
You are a leader of many
But your mercy is feint
You,
You are fast and never give up
You push til you make your goal
Stomping and pounding
And Never stopping,
Stomping and pounding
But you Never stop
You,
You are gold
Gold
My Gold
In my eyes
You dance with the wind
And in my mind
You are my Courage, my Power,
And my Pride.

Her: A Shadow, A Curse, A Prison
by Olivia Disant

She hurt me every time she spoke;
A never-ending shadow of sadness,
Cast upon my aching heart.
I tried to break free,
Tried to find an open door,
But found no escape, no refuge.
There's nothing you can do to save me,
Nothing that can break the curse.
I've fallen to the point of no return.
Even when I think it's over,
Another wave comes crashing down on me.
Wish I could leave, but I can't refuse.
I am my own captor,
There is always a way out,
But I never take it.
Without her I am empty,
But with her I am broken.
The torturous prison I can't escape.

Fragments of Truth
by Taylor DeLuca

Here I am again, in the same place I was yesterday.
Lying down and reassuring myself that I will be okay.
I believe the key to end the tragedy
is to not care about those who do not care for me.
Someone can say they care, but that does not assure they mean it.
Actions; the fact or process of doing something, typically to achieve an aim.
As pain and grief come and go throughout my life I've learned,
actions will speak louder than words. Always.
Words are not something you can count on.
They are just letters pieced together, ready to fall apart under a single breath.
The truth is something that can never be counted on.
It is strong yet fragile, just like us human beings.
We have those times where we are unbreakable,
but can utterly and completely collapse under just one word. Just one.
It tears at our insides and tries to get as profound as possible.
Our hearts slip out of beat for the sheerest second,
sadness rises from the pit of our stomachs,
and we feel the slightest ache which surrounds and indulges our entire bodies.
That is the most brief moment where the switch has to be flipped.
No more pain or constant sorrow. No more wondering or dejection.
No more despair or disappointment. No more anything.
The switch has been flipped.
All that's left is; a couple pieced together words.
All that's left is; insensibility and nothingness, dull eyes and pale face.
the switch has been flipped, we are now immune to uncontrollable emotions.

That Kind of Hell
by Lindsay McCommons

You don't know my story,
You don't know my name,
Yet you beat me, mock me,
Judge.
You call yourselves "Christians",
But is this what your God's like?
Does he hold grudges,
Constantly remind you of your mistakes?
Is he that shallow and rude,
Judging without knowing the whole story?
Because why would I want that?
Why would I want to follow
Someone so superficial?
Why would I want to spend eternity with them?
To live in that kind of Hell?
I'd rather
Burn
In flames.

Remembering
by Rachel Hartmann

New York City buses
Hats with pins and French accents
Streets and lights and smiles
Hands reaching to dance, reaching for the sky
Fingers running through paint and pages
Soft, warm, and tangy
Stockings left to dry and deep laughs
Why when the door opens do I think of you?
Why when I hear a voice do I think of you?
Pistachio ice cream
Invisible strings and scarves
Paint and charcoal and dimples
Eyes searching, eyes glimmering
Sweaters of cashmere and long afternoons
Math problems, letters, music
Why when the dog barks do I think of you?
Why when I look in the mirror do I think of you?
Bobby pins
Christmas lights, cushions, coffee, tea
Passion, fury, love
Last November and last December
Pastel colors, leather gloves, and good bread
Noses scrunching, noses running
My family and my life and me
And you.

Destiny
by Kyaijah Abdulahad

Our passion is a silent ache
Hush
Somewhat louder than the rest
Our thoughts are grey and opaque
Getting hard to catch my breath
In the grave, amongst us all
Laid my dreams and dignity
We continue to climb until we fall
But I enjoy the view I see
We crave the special. Schedules settle.
I am short of my precious vessel
Losing our mind, we're losing control
We hope that the path will be gentle.
I don't know where they're going
And they don't know where I'll be
Just follow the path and you'll be free
This is our destiny
Hush
This is our destiny

Who Am I?
by Christian Kotten

I am a brother, cousin, son, grandson, a student, a role model.
My friends are like a separate family,
but the people in my family are my best friends for life.
I am like any normal boy who has dreams.
But I dream to have, see, do, and become only the best,
not only for myself, but for others.
I want to help those who are down, bullied, different, stressed,
and give them a smile.
My dreams of being a role model for many,
someone to look up to, someone to help those who need it.
I want my words to spark inspiration and ideas within my followers.
I want my words to become a chain reaction where one person is inspired
to say my words to others and those others spread my words to many more.
The struggle and the chaos of battling a growth deficiency, ADHD,
and bullies all tore me down when I was young.
I was one of the few kids who stood out
but I still stand out ... but in a different way.
It was unbearable, but as I got older I have learned to move on.
Once you move on, and clear your mindset
of all the things that dragged you down, will then only make you stronger
and that will help you achieve what is wanted most in life.
Tune out all of the negativity and all of the bullies, and open up to those
who care, respect, and love you for who you are.
I am me.

The Polar Bear
by Shane Marshall

A bright white billiard storms the iceberg
A small white polar bear stands in fear, but the storm vanishes
The blazing sun, beams out from the clouds
It's too hot, temperatures skyrocket
The ice begins to melt
The polar bear is alone, crying and weeping
The ice slowly disappearing
Drips of water returning to the ocean
A slight cracking sound emerges
The noise strengthens then the cracks become visible
Slowly slicing the iceberg in half
The polar bear sadly is in the wrong place
A loud snap finishes the cut
The iceberg melted into little water droplets
The polar bear trapped, and alone
Sinks slowly into the dark abyss below
No way to swim or save itself
Sinks, sinks, sinks
Until it is gone for good

Stress
by Alanna Morse

I feel like the weight of the world is on my shoulders
I feel like a brick is pressing down on my stomach
Keeping the air from coming in
I feel like I can no longer go on, at least without breaking down
Frustration builds inside me, creeping up through my throat
Making an appearance throughout my daily life
I try to push it down, I try to hide it
To make it invisible, at least to everyone around me
Of course I can feel it, with every sudden move
With every decision I'm forced to make, with every task I'm given
Like something is burning inside me, charring my insides
Marking them with an anxious, unbearable feeling
Of course not present, not present on the outside, to the outside world
The outside, a shell of assurance that everything is fine
Putting on a show of happiness for the crowd you present to
But you know it's there
Present on the inside, you can feel the fire inside
They don't know, they don't suspect a thing
But you can feel it, you can feel it raring to come out
As the days go on, it's eating you alive
Gnawing at your flesh and well being
You try to push it down, you try the best that you can, you try and hide it
But every day it gets stronger, and every day you try to push it down
But it gets harder, and harder, and harder, and harder, and harder

Hindsight
by Wendy Moore

I know you're looking back at me, buried in your brain.
An "Oh, I remember that" moment to bring shame.
I bet you're looking down on me, because I am too!
There's no difference there, between me and you.
I don't know where you are,
but I sure hope it's not here.
I hope you ran so far,
that you couldn't feel the fear.
The truth? It's rather sad,
I'm sure you're still in bed,
just sitting in denial.
You'll be there until you're dead.
If we've never been better, then we've never been worse,
isn't it unfortunate, life cannot reverse.
I suppose it's my fault, I'm sorry that I did this,
I'm something to forget, a burden on your happiness.
I look up to you like I look up at the sun,
someday I'll float up and we will become one -
Even if it's false hope, it's what keeps me sane
So, I'll look for you, until we're the same.

Inherently Beautiful
by Alissa Hoover

Whether it be
the way she drops her offensive guard around them,
the way a small dimple becomes apparent when he smiles his true smile,
the way she ignites the whole room in laughter with her jokes,
the way he passionately serenades his pillow with songs of love,
the way her twinkling eyes speak a million words
when she can't say anything,
the way the golden morning sun catches in her hair,
the way his routine smiles reassure them that they'll be just fine,
the way he relentlessly gathers hope each lifeless day,
the way the college student, tired, stays up through the night
talking to the kid on the roof,
the way the child, lively, shapes a world to seize with their friends, or
the way he bares his soul to the paper, recounting every experience,
the way she gets lost in the celestial bodies,
wishing she could become a star herself,
the way the scars on their arms tell stories only they can read,
the way they cry every night to the moon, they tell their pain,
the way, you, with tears in your eyes, face every challenge,
in every aspect of life, there is beauty.
Despite all the hardships, I implore you to look, look and you'll see,
Humans are inherently beautiful,
You are beautiful.

The Terror
by Kennedy Blocher

I sat fit, in shock of what my mind was trying to catch.
As I sit at hand with this award that I obtain, and try to put my mind at unity.
I avail positivity as my ammunition.
As for I am lasting and at no hour shall I disjunction to the sounds of horror.

Lost In Music
by Alison "Sky" Benitez

The music plays
As his gaze
Evaporates my mind.
In the notes, I see
In the symphonies, I breathe
I've been stuck all this time.
But now the words rhyme.
His every memory,
My every melody,
Flutter and chime.
The power in the noise,
Just like his voice,
Lets me drift off into time.
While I was lost I found:
Only a piano could do this.
I sit and play just to realize,
I'm lost in the music.

The Test!
by Heaven Colōn

Heaven couldn't stop thinking about the test.
It was just so aggravating and infuriating, she was vexed.
But she could never forget to try her best!
That morning, Heaven encountered a test, such a mess.
She found herself feeling rather depressed.
But she couldn't stop thinking about the test.
Later, Heaven was shocked by a request.
She tried to focus on the rest, but she could never forget the test.
Ivory tried to distract her from the test,
said it was time to start thinking about the rest.
But still, Heaven couldn't stop thinking about the test.
Heaven took action for the best, she made herself feel less depressed.
The test was like a toxic shard,
But she could never forget what Ivory said and tried her best.
Heaven tried her best on the rest, but still her mind was a mess.
Heaven couldn't stop thinking about the test.
But she could never forget she tried her best!

Painful Love
by Kaitlyn Copeland

I used to think that life was good.
You were the highlight of my day.
I've always heard that love is patient and love is kind.
But instead, you abused the love I gave you.
Once you left, my heart broke in two.
And since you are no longer around, all I can think is love is pain.

Muddy Sorrow
by Lucas Vladimiroff

I walked into the muddy basin,
My boots shone black and brown.
My fellow friends were there and sank in,
So there my good friends drown.
"Where must they be," they all came shouting,
Our suits all red with blood.
We sat there with the silent mouthing,
"They all fell in the mud."
I stood there in the heartfelt houses,
With empty bed and chair.
I heard the building's silent spouses,
In one gigantic fair.
So we all come up in black and white,
And offer up the tears.
But what is there is out of sight,
And there we find our fears.

How to Dance with the Moon
by Anna Kipp

When the moon is full and the clouds part, open a window that's near.
Make sure the family is tucked away and nobody can hear.
Look up to the sky and smile brightly so he can see your face.
He'll send a cloud down to you, to send you up to space.
The fluffy, white pillow will make you want to sleep.
And through the night, though with his smile, his loneliness makes him weep.
Most nights he sits, sad and alone, waiting for you to come.
So do not waste time or make him wait, this task must soon be done.
Don't get too tiresome, you won't want the rest.
You will need that energy to go about at your best.
Up you'll go, to the heavens, make sure to hold on tight.
No tears should wander, it's just the sky, there is no need for fright.
Once you reach the stars above, he will take your hand.
Off you'll go on a smooth path, and hear the moonlight band.
The song so slow with, peace and love, it'll make you want to sing.
Then all night long, you'll be with the moon, dancing on Saturn's rings.

BMX Life
by Nathan Byler

I could be spending time inside like other kids
but instead I am on a BMX bike
everyone doesn't respect me
it's very expensive just to do some tricks
but it's better than being inside playing video games
living their fake reality while I am trying to make dreams come true

Hospital Stay
by Scotia Foose

White beat-up walls
2 white thin blankets
Blue and white gowns
Beds glued to the ground
Being watched 24/7
Soggy food in Styrofoam containers
Fenced blacktop
Medicine time
Quiet time
Don't forget the therapy sessions
Doctors that get paid too much to not care about you
Girls who don't want to leave
Fights
Within themselves
With other girls
Who will get the needles tonight?

The Forever Marathon
by Nicole Farrell

Running across the track with billions behind and ahead
Long time ago, I rolled outta my bed
The forever marathon is where we at, we can't stop
One day, you think you gon' come out on top
Winners are the ones that bleed cash and have a star on the track
Anyone competes, mansion or a shack
The terrain is always switching, but we can't predict the land
But some, they quit early by their own hands
Every passing year, my feet grow tired of this winding road
Yet I keep on going, humid or cold
Time runs faster the more I age, before I know my hair grays
Body runs on, but do I leave or stay?
I gotta stay, that's the program in our bodies shouting out
That's the point of this race, what it's about
One day, a racer could kill me or imma fall to the floor
My laps are done, and I can't race no more

Heavy
by Miranda Brandon

Today I feel chemical.
Some days my body will rationalize the feeling
and my brain can recognize it's all within itself;
it's all in my head.
Other days it's so heavy,
it feels as if all of my thoughts
could pour right out of my ears.
It's just one of those days.

Nature Is Life
by Preston Astrow

The sun shines on a new day.
The autumn leaves fall to the glistening bright ground
As the sun breaks through the clouds.
The birds awake and sing their song,
The one they spend their life perfecting.
The wind bellows a burst
As the trees shake and the leaves blow.
The bees glide from flower to flower.
The deer gallop around the curvy hills.
Fish navigate through a rapid stream.
As the sun falls under the orange horizon
And the moon fades into place, life stays dormant.
Life awaits, under the pale bright light,
For the sun to start the world again
And for nature to take its course.

The Land I Grew Up On
by Abigail Brown

The land curves around the river
The leaves rustle in the wind
This is the field I used to run in;
When I see the old man upon the tractor
I wave my hand,
so he lifts his hat.
Birds fly across the sky and swoop down to the water
The smell of cut grass in the summertime
While the winter brings the fresh smell of pine
With a white snowy glow
I stand in the middle of field
With my eyes closed
I feel the crisp breeze against my face
This is where I have always felt in my place
On the land I grew up on

Roses In Springtime
by Leianna Mckeever

Ruby red petals are dropped
With rain, the deep
Red roses rest against each other.
The raindrops leap from one red
Petal to another. Ruby red
Petals and emerald green leaves
Sway gently, and quietly in the
Small breeze.

Farmers of America
by Hailie Whetstone

You may not realize how hard they work
Waking up every morning to work in the dirt
Putting food on our tables
When they are able
Working when they are sick
Working hard even though they are not rich
The Farmers of America have a hard life
Working every day and night
Slinging bails by hand from an old wagon
To working on an old farm truck
Farmers work hard
We may not see it
We might not believe it
If it wasn't for farmers we would starve
The Farmers of America work hard

Lock and Key
by Jimmy Takats

For what is and what was it was.
The clock continues to tick, as I'm told that time's arrow only marches forward,
but it seems that I feel nothing towards that.
it seems that the world continues to pass me by,
that with or without me the world still spins,
I guess it is hard for me to realize
that I am nothing but a speck in the grand scheme of things,
that I am not that important.
Am I that important? To whom do I matter to? To where do I belong?
If home is where the heart is, why do I not feel secure anywhere?
Where am I going with my journey and can I even call this a journey,
why do I feel the way I do and why does it burn my soul
to know I do not possess the answers to all the world's questions.
As I struggle with reflection the man in the mirror is still a blur,
but I guess to me that is all I am worth.

The Fire
by Jenna Lestage

I am the light in the dark,
The hot amber glow upon the ground.
I am the one who dances on coals
On the ashes of those I've burnt.
I was the hope of times long past,
Needed, treasured, fought for.
I was warmth, home, safety, passion.
Now I am cast aside.
I will be here if you want,
But if you need me, I will consume.
For I am destruction, anger and wrath.
I am the fire who used to have your back.

Broken Pieces
by Joei Lipscomb

I always tend to have the feeling that I'm in the shadows.
Knowing that I will never fit in like everyone else.
I am the second choice if I'm even a choice at all.
Most of the time I feel like a fragile glass,
The only problem is I'm on the edge ready to break into millions of pieces.
I tend to love someone more than I love myself.
I get my heart broken and the worst part is I can't hate the person,
I still care and think about them when I get upset.
Most of the time I put on a smile and block the tears from falling.
My world is like a giant bubble ready to pop.
The only question I'm asking myself is,
"What piece of my heart do I follow when it is in a million?"

Life Vests
by Cassandra Johnson

My friends and I are all drowning in the same ocean.
We grasp at each other trying to hold fast to what we know will never leave.
But if we're all drowning how can we possibly save each other?
I kick and gasp for breath as I try to hold them up.
Intertwined, we slip deeper under the surface
as we remember that everyone leaves us.
Dad, mom, friends, the boys that held our hearts until they got bored.
No one can stay forever, so who's to say that we must stay?
But we do stay. We stay for each other,
because we know that if one of us drowns the others will soon follow behind.
So we kick and gasp, fighting for every single breath we take.
We give away our life vests to ensure that the others will be okay.
But in an ocean full of drowning people
there aren't enough life vests to save us all.

A Mistake Waiting To Happen
by Bryce Suders

You ever think of what not to say?
How the words itching to be told can never be?
How ironic ... words killing the writer
hurtful knowing that the thoughts on your mind
would destroy the only thing that brings you joy,
is the one thing taking away your joy.
I'm a poem ... I leave myself heartbroken.
but what does that make you?
Don't love me. I'm just a poem ... I'll leave you heartbroken

Growing Up
by Madison McFarland

An excited little girl lies in bed; Dreams of sugarplums dance in her head.
"Goodnight," mom whispers.
Then off she goes, Off to the land where sugarplums dance.
A pretty dress hangs on her closet door; Waiting for the evening to come.
Finally, it's time.
The girl puts on the dress, and off she goes;
Off to the land where sugarplums dance.
The show begins. A little girl watches in awe.
Jump, Twirl, Run; All on the tips of their toes.
Off in the land where sugarplums dance.
The show is over, And an awe-inspired girl lies in bed,
Dreams of sugarplums dancing in her head.
Then off she goes, Off to the land where sugarplums dance.
"Please, mommy, please!" a little girl cries, Days and weeks pass before finally;
A little girl has something new on her door:
Leotard, tights, and brand new ballet shoes.
Off to the studio, off to train for the very first time.
Everything had a new feeling.
Mirrors; excitement, Barres; support, Floors; joy,
A little girl; unbelief of where she is.
Four years later, a little girl goes to a new studio.
Suddenly, things start to change.
The feelings she had before are not there.
The feelings are different, more intense.
Off to discover new feelings. This time these emotions were more enchanting.
Mirrors; enhancement, Barres; enthusiasm, Floors; energy, A little girl; passion.
Some other things had changed as well,
The stage was no longer just another surface; It was a whole other world
Full of emotion, passion, excitement, expression. Off to express, not to impress.
Later on in her life, a little girl not so little anymore, Will graduate high school.
She'll move on with dreams as high as the sky.
No matter where life takes her, she knows she'll always be loved.
Then off she goes, off to begin a life of her own.

The Thought Scar
by Garrett Talbott

Scars do not heal
They stay like a burden
Never to leave you
We all wish we had lovers like scars
They would never leave in a lifetime
But instead, lovers cause scars
We all have scars no matter the cause
Mental scars, physical scars
None are too little for all
We all have these scars and pains
You wonder how you'd lose them
Why did they leave and pain you
You think the cure for these scars is more love
No, there's just more scars and disappointment above
The cure for this is lust
No, there's just loneliness and anger
Maybe it could be more love
Wrong as always
You'd have to be dimwitted to think that
So then you just sit with those scars and cover them all with lies
And again this false cycle occurs

The Phoenix
by Melody Lateer

I act like the words don't hurt me,
I laugh it off as if I find it funny,
I pretend I don't care,
As if it doesn't affect me.
But it hurts, okay?
It breaks me down piece by piece,
I already rip myself apart,
I don't need you as another reminder of all my mistakes and faults.
You put me under a microscope and through a magnifying glass,
Until the heat of your judgmental gaze and words you say,
Light me on fire so you can watch me burn.
You laugh at the ashes left behind as it's all that's left of me,
The flames that have died leaving nothing but a shell of who I was,
The ashes you watch fly through the air as the wind scatters it.
But like a phoenix I will be renewed as I emerge from those ashes,
To live once again and start anew built off those ashes as my foundation to rise,
I will use them as a reminder to motivate myself for the awakening as I ignite.
So say what you want but those sparks you see glow as I disintegrate,
Those are embers that indicate
the passion and strength of my spirit I will use to revive,
Into something more beautiful with strength you never knew.

Glorious
by Olivia Payne

She may have fallen
She is stronger than she knows
She will rise once more

Wings
by Sarah Huang

I am weak
I am strong
I don't float
But yet I fly
Who am I?
I am your pair of invisible wings
Made up of memories
Happy and sad alike
Each one adding a feather
To your beautiful, invisible wings
I hope these wings will continue to grow
With beautiful memories
And fly you
Up
Up
Up
Where you can see the whole world

Pink Bath Salts
by Emma Race

I am fading from this world.
A kaleidoscope of colors draining through my fingertips,
dripping onto the pure white tile.
I collect the dye in buckets,
then I drink it,
hoping it will return the stained glass shades to my body.
I am sitting in a puddle of my own pigmentation.
I stick my face to the floor and try to slurp up as much of the liquid as I can.
My lungs are always overflowing with paint,
spilling into my esophagus,
creeping its way up my throat and dribbling from my lips.
But no matter how much acrylic I guzzle down,
my heart still remains uninhabited by iridescence,
devoid of any comfort and satisfaction.
I fill the porcelain bathtub with the color from my carcass
so I can marinate in a rainbow of my own depression,
letting it seep into my pores.

Falling To Spring
by Anushka Khandelwal

I love to see the colorful leaves
Falling off the maple tree
As it gives a sense of something new to erupt in the spring
The air now is crisp and cold with snowflakes on the tree
Goosebumps are set up to go
Hands are rubbing to hug the warmth of cocoa
Waiting for time to pass, to melt and welcome new budding leaves of the tree.
A rainbow is on its way to paint the buds with colors
Giving a sense that spring is here.

Never Give Up
by Amber Houle

Never give up
Always be hopeful
Things will change
If you give up
You will never know
What could have been
What you could have done
You will never know your true destiny
You will never know what you're truly capable of
You will never know your full potential
So, stay hopeful
Keep your chin up
And no matter what,
Never, ever give up

The Bone Garden
by Logan Shives

Red fronds coiled under a harsh sun
Leaves frayed a bright vermillion awaiting a late autumn
Curled towards the light for nourishment in waning days
Drinking sunrises and sunsets before a skeletal season
Locking its treasure in a spiked wooden vault
This bush stared into the open horizon for years
And not yet will it shrivel under the sun's wrathful gaze
It lives for this, locked in its earthen pedestal home,
Rooted in the backlot bone garden, thriving
Yet under this crimson crown of thorns is nestled an unlikely gift
Wound about a brown dried husk
Was a little spider-woven wind chime
Slowly twirling in the thick tranquil air -
Waiting to ring clearly for the cold winds that come

Soccer Time
by Ashley M. Arriaga

I stand in the far back
left, not in the middle
in the position I love, outside left back.
I wait till it's my
TIME,
Time to show my skill,
Time to be fierce and aggressive,
Time to win that ball,
Time to make that ball yours,
Time to help a teammate by making that amazing perfect pass,
Time to shoot that ball with might,
Time to win.

Tacos
by Graciana Dorries

I love tacos,
They make me go psycho,
I add my meats,
But I add no beets,
I like to add cheese,
It would hurt if there were bees,
The taco isn't complete without salsa,
Though I don't like it in my pasta,
I prefer my pasta plain,
I wonder, do they do that in Spain?
Now I'm getting off topic,
But who would want to stop it?

The Chase
by Victoria Frangione

There she lies on her side,
Likely dreaming of being outside.
She often runs and jumps towards the trees,
Her eyes point in the direction of what she sees.
Rabbits and squirrels lurk about,
Her excitement is evident without a doubt.
The chase begins with a flying bound,
But the squirrel scurried off, and the rabbit dove into the ground.
To her dismay, the chase came to an end,
But luckily for her, she'll always have a friend.
That's because she is my dog whom I love so,
I know our friendship will only grow.

Purple Fog
by Olivia Vice

Quarrelling bees.
Roving woman.
Unsure echoes of purple waves
Pervaded the empty impression of me.
Where have you gone?
Do you lay amid the weeping lilies,
Beneath a wrinkled and weary tree?
Do birds exhale their trembling whispers
Above the soil which has taken you in?
All of you.
I still see you. Dancing in the fog.
Like something poured.

Wakeful Restlessness
by Irina Zhang

Like a bird of December
I hide awake with no sleep to welcome
Under a moonlit haze
Rattles a mind whose wish is to wonder
Eyes wide
To see the time
Eyes lined
To clatter through the mind
And when the sun escapes
The mind becomes obsolete
Surrendering to the stillness
Of just one night

Silence
by Sabrina Harrison

The shadowy figure stalks the hall,
It passes by spreading terror to all,
Weeping and wailing fills the air,
As the mysterious creature deepens its stare.
As people fell, no more was said,
Their hearts forever filled with dread,
As the creature finished its final hike,
The fear hits me like a steel spike.
As the figure pulled back its hood with a croak,
Its form was revealed from under its cloak,
Then suddenly with a great start, I awoke,
What I saw above me, almost gave me a stroke.

Man
by James Pickering

I have lived a thousand lives;
I have died a thousand deaths.
I have opened my heart to few;
and have been welcomed by fewer.
I have been pierced by my own knives;
and cursed by the breath of others.
I have made the world anew;
but it has been replaced by one newer.
Plagued by loneliness but
unbeknownst to longing
Hounded by another's demands,
yet unable to fulfill them.
And within my heart is joy shut
a Pandora's Box to me belonging
Creating life with mine own hands
never belonging, and never foreign
This is the life that I have lived,
These are the deaths that I have died
This is who I am,
This is the race of man.

G?d
by Gabrielle Wick

A spoon clangs against a fine china cup
as it paddles through broiling liquid.
It shatters centuries of silence.
A well crafted spoon, an elegant tea cup,
as beautiful as the being wielding them.
Elegant and well crafted,
sculpted to perfection and molded by time.
Love sanded in His gentle curves.
Sadness etched the wrinkles into His brow.
Wisdom deepened His already endless eyes.
The edges of the universe lay behind them.
Ever-expanding, ever-present,
His mind filled with galaxies none would ever see
aside from Himself,
so He remains silent,
as none could comprehend His mind.
How lonely it must be
to know the secrets of everything,
only to look into the expanse of nothingness
and gently nurse His tea.

Untouchable
by Derek McCardell

Success is not as it seems
Life is not a trip
We may shout and scream
And think the world is ours
But for as long as we are present on this Earth
Love
Success
Excitement
Joy
Is not in our reach
We are stuck within the walls
Played like a little game
It is a routine
Can you not see?
They are untouchable
Nothing to lose
We are struggling
In pain
But no one is there
To take us away.

Depressed and Repressed
by Jaiden Hodge

Unheard cries and lifeless screams.
A sinister evil behind the scenes.
It grapples on and drains your hope.
Until the time comes to tie the rope.
Its dark shadow looms over the soul.
And in time, it shall take its toll.
Isolated within the shadows.
As if drowning within the shallows.
The pain excruciating.
The loneliness unbearing.
We sometimes live only feeling depressed.
With all our emotions bottled and repressed.
Those who survive, live a life of sorrow.
Their mindset focused on there being no tomorrow.
Morbid sensations and the thoughts of rejection,
Course through our veins like the source of an infection.
If only people could see that maybe,
All the depressed need is a friend.
If only they could see,
That the depressed are all nearing a grim end.

Ode To the Beach
by Samantha Roxburgh

Beach oh beach
You are so nice
With ocean and soft sand
They are treasures alike
Beach oh beach
You're quiet as a pin
That helps the world calm
All through the thick and thin
Beach oh beach
You're crashing waves
The taste and smell of salt
Will last for days
Beach oh beach
People from near and far
All agree that you are
Brighter than a star
Beach oh beach
I love you so
So please do not
Ever go

Forever
by Chauncey Higgins

From the day I was born I've been both warm and real cold
I'll take something new and make it grow old
Before you realize I hit you it'll be a slap in the face
You'll be looking back at the years you easily misplaced
Some call me a mystery, some call me a race
Every one knows me from Cali to Maine
Some people, they read me and they learn of the past
At the moment I'm slow but from the future I'm fast
I can stretch out a moment to every extent
I can be like a gift and they call me a present
And before you know it you'll be counting your days
I'm simple like colors but complex like a maze
I always move forward but never go back
You want to know who I am, let's sit down for a chat
You want me to be nice but I'm never so kind
You already know my name, I'm none other than Time
I'm loud but quiet and live life like a mime
I'm long when you live but I'm short when you die
I can be blunt like a rock or as sharp as a knife
Some say I give life meaning, but I give meaning to life

Where Do We Really Go?
by Kira Christensen

When we open up our phones,
Where do we really go?
There are so many apps,
And so much we don't know.
Some look for the bad things,
And some just watch a show.
Why'd they create the internet?
Well I might never know.
Most say it's a distraction,
I'm stuck on interaction.
Not everybody is good,
Most can be tragic.
This is a big topic,
Most people move past it.
What I wonder is,
Why everyone has it.
A phone.
But most people don't know.
Like when we open up our phones,
Where do we really go?

No Goodbyes
by Katie Rose

They say life has its ups and downs,
but what if your life just spins around?
Same truths, same lies, yet no goodbyes.
For that I am quite grateful.
Yet I keep on walking,
Among the dead and the living.
No one can truly be gone,
unless you have forgotten their song,
they will live on.
Through tears, through memories.
I'm not ready to begin my song,
it will truly be short, not very long.
My life is split with love and hate,
although the love can never break.
It may just slowly fade away.
Here I will watch from this bay,
as the sun falls with its rays.
That is when I truly form.
For at night,
I am free to roam.

Light
by Morgan Ferguson

The sun issued an ultimatum
To the land below:
"Reclaim the light of antiquity,
Or perish in your woe."
The poet sought the answer
In the void beneath the skin;
They saw light in fervent passion,
In focusing instead on fleeting grins.
But the genius, with his intellect,
Knew knowledge was the key;
He fashioned monuments and manuscripts
Of present ingenuity.
And the king ignored the both of them,
Conquering distant, shining shores—
To smite the brutes that kept them
From the golden light of yore.
"You fools!" proclaimed the sun,
Perceiving all that had transpired.
"The light you see is not salvation,
But your funeral pyre!"

Societies Are the Whispers
by Jessie Miller

How have we come so far,
But lost so much along the way?
People have whispered in my ear all my life.
It was all so subtle I unconsciously heard it all.
They formed me into who I am today.
Someone I do not want to be.
They mold us into fantasies,
Putting expectations on us, limiting us from who we could be.
Societies are those whispers.
I do not want to be what society wants me to be.
I will say out loud what I want when society says no, be quiet.
I will act as I please.
I will dress as I please.
I will eat what I please.
Your opinion does not matter,
There is only ONE opinion I truly care about.
So you can call me what you want,
But I will never conform.
I will stand strong for what I believe,
And society can't stop me.

Great Grandpop Peter Boruch
by John Krwawicz

It was at a young age
When we lost Grandpop Peter.
He had suddenly died
And I felt like a griever.
We started to cry
When we lost Grandpop Peter.
He had died from cancer
And we lost a true leader.
A WWII veteran
He wanted to be known for.
Until the doctor said no
He would see doctors no more.
His ashes are in a box
And I visit them often.
And when I see the box
My mood becomes softened.
We talk about grandpop
So we don't forget him.
When we talk about Peter
Our moods become grim.

Combustion
by Amanda Jones

Beautiful from a distance,
But when you got too close it burned.
Burns engraved across your fingertips,
Your lips, and your mind.
But he was so stunning, you could never stay away.
You tried to change him,
Tried to make him love you
The same way you loved him.
You tried it all, but everything you did he consumed,
And made him grow even stronger.
He craved the attention,
And you kept giving it to him.
Because maybe one day,
He'd finally see something in you.
But he never did, and you realized he never would.
So you and your heart burned out,
Yet he stayed raging, looking for someone else
To keep him ignited.
The boy I loved,
Fire.

Silence
by Emmalynne Sherman

My mind is a hive,
Full of bees,
Buzzing in a never-ending fashion.
The only way to calm my bees,
Is a way deemed "attention-seeking".
When my bees become too loud and insulting,
I have found a way to quiet them.
When silence carves into my flesh,
The bees' thirst for heartbreak falters.
But again,
The bees come back,
Each bearing a new insult.
Again,
Full of shame,
Do I dig another grave of despair.
Each new bee comes with a new set of stings to torture me.
But one day a dragonfly will appear,
To fight off the bees' stingers.
And until the bees are no more,
My hive becomes a happy silence.

Perfect Delight
by Kelsey Hart

Butterflies flutter and swirl around,
Suddenly you forget all you have learned.
The nerves attack you until you drown,
All of us are frantically concerned.
We walk on to stage and the magic hits,
The spotlight, the crowd, it all just fits.
The music blares and you fall into a trance,
Everything's perfect, we graciously dance.
We spin, jump, and turn in perfect sync.
The crowd absorbs it all, not wanting to blink.
We pour our emotions out on the stage,
Hearts are pounding straight through one's rib cage.
The time flies by, and quickly comes to an end.
You wish and wish just to do it again.
The nerves became fuel letting nothing contend,
To the feeling and glow from the stage, our best friend.
We left our heart on the stage, without a doubt
And heard the loud crowd, as we all just looked out.
We took our bows and left the bright light,
Holding onto that feeling of perfect delight.

Where Are You Going?
by Elise Schmitt

What are you worth
In the place you call home?
Are you a priceless treasure
Where you are going to go?
Or are you worth just enough
To help you get by?
Do you lie wide awake
Counting debts every night?
Where you are going,
How are you paid?
Is your work valued
Or do you waste away?
The hours you spend working
Is it time well spent?
Or do your valiant efforts
Barely make rent?
Where you come from, friend
Are you special, loved and free?
If not, know at day's end
You can always stay with me

We Are the Lions
by Amy Smith

We are the lions, who built this home
We are the one whose bodies moan
Long hard and weathered this path we stalked
Forever remembering the ones we left behind and lost
We are the outsiders in this narrative we craft
Away from where we came from, we look back and laugh
But behind the worn smiles and tired eyes
There is a story behind them which dormant lies
We are the survivors of the tragedies
The ones which echo and haunt our memories
But a long way we've come from that beautiful but agonizing hell
A heaven we have built here, and our tale do we tell
We are the fighters with graces bold
Brash and loud, our strengths unfold
We have fought for our freedom and won
We outnumber all of them, fifteen to one
We are the lions, who built this home
And no longer across this earth do we roam
Together we stand, bruised but not broken
And this is our anthem which we have spoken

Apples of Life
by Samantya Sackey

Roses are red
Violets are blue
Life is a sweet ride
A fable I was told too
After being told too many lies
You feel the tears on your face begin to dry
Dry, dry, as they flow like a melodic tune in a lullaby
But they are nothing but sweet
Oh my sweet tears of rage
Tears, tears, oh so many tears
These tears resemble dew drops
Tears, tears, these rampant tears have never stopped
My heart is so heavy
I want to rid myself of this feeling but my shattered heart won't let me
I reside in the dark because the light just tends to burn me
Hiding away from this inevitable reality
Probably drown myself in this self-hated ink
My family and friends are my last link
Last link to a joyous life

My Hue
by Emma Morey

I am from red roses and gravestones,
And from a broken family missing our angel.
I am from long lonely nights,
From overthinking to death wishing.
I am from loving parents, who struggle.
I am from my quiet brother's loneliness,
And from slow rolling tears.
From the soft wind singing her name.
I am from police car sirens and gory details.
I am from funeral homes and closed caskets,
From long lost souls to hearts that are no longer whole.
I am from the spitting image of someone who was adored,
From getting mistaken as the family black sheep.
I am from haunting dreams.
I am from feelings out of my control,
And from overdoses and motorcycle crashes.
I am from smoking stalks and illegal drugs,
From my maternal last name.
I am from my mother's dear dead sister, who sadly passed away.

Winter
by Emily Oswald

Crisp air bites at my cheeks,
While a chilling breeze yanks at my hair.
A heavy, bulky coat keeps me warm,
And my wool scarf flows in the wind.
The snow falls softly around me,
Falling in flakes no bigger than a grain of rice.
The grass hides behind a blanket of white,
Like a child playing hide and seek.
Bright, colorful holiday lights reflect off the new visitor,
Making every distraction disappear.
This season is a favorite of many,
Yet an enemy of others.
It arrives in full force, fearing none,
And leaves like a friend.
A sad goodbye,
But hopeful for another visit.
Surrounded by the warmth of the season,
I hear the faint whisper ...
Winter.

Salvation
by Emeli Dion

A single person haunts her thoughts, sitting on her shoulder.
She shivers when she gets touched, in fear of being hurt by another.
Her eyes shed tears late into the night, she sometimes is overcome by fright.
A woman's body is her own, one to be held by a blanket of security.
Her world was on fire,
each step burning into her memory like a plague of despondency.
She felt trapped, as though she were under water,
But the water was dark and murky, with no clear direction to follow.
Yet a light shone one day, and she swam to the top.
The fire was out, the burning coal no longer hot.
She found saviors, people to pull her out of the pit.
Her body grew limp with gratitude,
For those who saved her helped her escape
The very place she thought she'd be stuck in forever.
Some days are worse but some days are better.
She walks through life as if it were a field full of flowers.
She is now free, and has places to be.
She found herself once more.

The Hunt
by Heather Lipari

As I'm walking in the forest
Quick before my eyes
Barely catching my attention
Leaves and twigs crunching with its every step
A deer
Starting to slow down
Scoping its surroundings
Searching for fresh, ripe berries
So innocent, wouldn't harm you
But I watch from a distance
The deer spots me, stares at me for awhile
Watching very closely,
Suddenly
Bang!
It goes silent
Not a single sound
The sweet deer
Now will not see the light of day again

Storm of the Sea
by Lyndsey Persampire

I close my eyes while sitting on the coastline
It is about to storm
I can feel the waves hitting my skin
The power of the waves pulsing through me
My soul longs to know the secrets of the sea.
What's really out there?
There is so much that has not been explored.
The sea hides the unknown.
I long to swim out there and never come back
I start to walk into the rough ocean current
I feel like a magnetic pull is pulling me to walk deeper and deeper
The sea mist splashing against my face
The cold wind blowing through my hair.
The light grey skies overhead
Lightning strikes
At that sound I dive deep into the water.
Longing to explore the depths of the sea
And after that I will not be swimming back up ever again.

Roller Coaster
by Jayden LaCoe

My progress is a roller coaster
Going up to the heavens one second
then down to the deepest depths
These depths get
deeper and deeper
Each one darker than the last
I think this one is blackout
no light to be seen
trying to climb back up
is a clanging, broken mechanism
Struggling
through what seems impossible
Then I go up
up
up
again
before falling even deeper
than I have ever yet

The Race
by Luke McKenna

When he puts me on, I know my time has come,
to get in the water, and show them what I'm made of.
He jumps in the water, and I feel the water shatter,
he says, "It really doesn't matter,"
but I feel the pressure boiling from under.
The sight of the competitors, from the left to the right,
may make me anxious, but I know the future is bright.
As I move from one end of the pool to the other, I think ...
Maybe this time, it's my chance.
Maybe this time, we'll advance.
Maybe this time, he'll do that little dance.
When the race has finished, I hear his teammates scream,
and I know that we have just achieved his dream.
Like a soldier coming back from war,
I see his teammates run up to him and say,
"That's what you've been working at."
And in the wise words of Cardi B, I hear him say,
"I like it like that."

She's Broken
by Mary Teresa Comerate

She's broken
With eyes that paint colors of black and white
with a heart that's only ever felt hate
a mind that can't give the right answers
With cracked ribs
an' lungs that can't expand
With a mouth that only hands out lies
Her skin covered in the color of black and blue
An' words that cut like a knife
Emotions only being a word that's used to express pain
Love ever only being a word she's heard an' never felt
Friend being a word she uses to describe the drowning depths of her mind

Eternal Winter
by Isadora Maksym

Snow covering dense, Brobdingnagian trees,
Shading the ground from the fresh morning light,
Altering it into crisp darkness.
Two glacier, icy eyes peering from whipped meringue bushes
once flush with life, and now forever frozen in eternal stillness.
Snow gracefully showering down from the heavens
like slender ballerinas performing the Nutcracker.
The sound of icicles crashing onto the icy pavement,
shattering like porcelain china, scattering into a myriad of razor-sharp pieces.
A crisp gush of arctic air chilling everything in sight,
Altering everything into perfect stillness,
Cold and motionless 'til the end of time.

Paper Lines
by Ethan Staudte

The one escape from all our minds is written down on paper lines.
No search for help from all our hells, we just stay trapped inside our cells.
A cage of all our mental ills is masked by other pointless thrills.
These walls are weak to heavy pills that none of us has sought.
For once we start we cannot stop, our souls have thus been bought.
No psychology or pharmacy, cry all of us in time.
Our therapy is poetry, our thoughts are told in rhyme.
From in our minds to paper lines and then in time reverse.
We pour out feelings cryptically revealing them in verse.
Until one day we all go mad, when everything is dead and sad.
Our stories told within these things, our poems that another sings,
The morbid truth poetry binds, our lives confined to paper lines.

Jesus
by Owen Czebiniak

Jehovah, God
Elohim, the living God
Savior, redeemer of the world
Unending, beginning and the end
Son of God, one in three of the holy trinity

Natural Accessories
by Hannah Messer

She was Eirene on earth.
Pure grace, she grew wild thyme in her hair.
The roots reached down into her core.
Her tears formed the oceans,
pulling whole tides with her heart.
The light in her eye
created blazing fires,
conviction that swept whole nations.
She opened her gates
to anyone who bared witness to her beauty.
A gift unto the world,
She sheltered all she touched.
And still, she lived for herself.
An act of self-love, an act of warfare.
She was my mother.

Sheep Ruminating In a Field
by Alexander Lee

I gaze at them
As they mindlessly feed
They relax
All spread out
Munching on grass
Then suddenly
I notice sheep disappearing
Leaving trails of cries for help
Only to notice patches of blood
Scared for their lives
They start to disperse
Running aghast
And jumping over fences
Only to find less and less sheep
And more ponds of blood

Just a Downgrade
by Fiona Hogan

Beautiful face.
Porcelain skin.
Perfect teeth.
Gorgeous body.
Superior intelligence.
Empathetic personality.
Just right in every way.
But one flaw lurks.
A shadow hidden by perfection.
Growing larger,
growing darker,
day by day,
consuming my perfect pale skin.
Intelligence suppressed,
and personality twisted.
But beauty remains,
perfect and untouched.
Like an empty doll,
crying invisible tears.
Sorry, but I'm just a downgrade.

I Am
by John C. DiBella, III

I am from a hospital in Huntington, New York
I am from a family of veterans and police
I am from a family of loving people
I am from the greater outdoors
I am from a family of vacationers
I am a golfer and coin collector,
a philanthropist and historian
I am a lover of the city
I am a roller coaster and water park enthusiast
I want to be a sailor in the US Navy
I want to go to Annapolis Naval Academy
I want to be a police officer
I want to live in the farm country and the wilderness
I want to have a Golden Retriever and a German Shepherd
I want to live a long and fun-filled life

Imagination
by Desireé Deery

Hazel;
Girl 6 years
Red hair that wants to be brown
Always bouncing in pigtails
Amber brown eyes
With the ability to only see positivity
Not old enough to work
Old enough to know what she wants to do
With her long and meaningful life
3'8 not enough to reach the top shelf
Without a stool
She tries anyways
Can be found climbing trees
Or running around a field
Pretending she wasn't alone
Last seen trying to paint the stars
With her fingers and dreams
If you see her
Tell her to not be afraid
Tell her dinner is ready

Rainy Day
by Fiorella Merriman-Mendez

Rain pours outside my window,
The sky seems to be sad,
Longing for stolen sunlight
That it did once have.
It cries for broken daydreams,
That litter earth's green ground.
It cries for those who suffer,
And through the wind carries on their sound.
It mourns for those words that'll never be written,
Those voices that will never sing,
For those that before they could even take flight
Already had broken wings.
So while we refuse to show our emotions,
The rain lets out for us what we cannot reveal,
Helping to remind us we're human
And reminding us of what we feel.

Congress
by Alex Wadsworth

C - checks and balances to the judicial and executive branch
O - official representatives of the states
N - negotiations between parties
G - general elections held periodically
R - right and left wing points of view
E - elected representatives gather
S - senate and the house of representatives make up the 2 chambers
S - speakers present their ideas to the floor

Separation
by Alyssa King

Waking up with the wind running through our house
feeling the cold spring breeze on my skin
the fresh roses planted outside were as sweet as candy
As I go outside and pick the delicious blueberries from spiky bush
Screaming and fighting aroused from inside
And it suddenly stopped when I walked back inside
my mother making Sunday dinner had stopped
my father watching football ended
And so did the family that laid within
It is my fault consistently ran through my mind
But I was told things just take time
It embarked inquiry and impacted the injury
Although the heart will never be completely filled
it consumes every piece to fit it in along the way

Mo(u)rning
by Ashley Barletta

The chill of upstairs and sour sun rays
that do not melt the snow, but polar ice caps
dazzle dusty curtains; the sniffling blanket— a trap,
pine eyes bloom and focus their gaze.
Stale limbs scuff their everyday maze,
and jaded lips swill the same old sap,
numb windowpanes finally unwrap
to unravel Earth's pearly raw glaze.
Pollution hustles along like black blazing cloud,
a vacant city road is failed to be plowed.
Crimson cheeks without heat frown 'neath scarf made of wool,
but the blush on her heart has made him a fool.
So the curtains stay open, the sun can be loud,
but pollution remains— too young and too proud.

The One
by Alexandra Williams

The one
The one girl that needs extra help
The one that always gets bullied
The one that can't stand up for herself
The one that sits at lunch by herself
The one that cries herself to sleep at night
We all know that person inside
And if it hasn't happened to you yet
It will
Because the bully's name is
Reality

The Quiet Lake of the Night
by Mario Giordano

He made a ripple,
In the quiet lake of the night.
Stars, meanwhile, inscribed a scalding fresco in the sky,
Massacring the darkness.
He pondered many things during his swim,
And came to conjecture as he looked upward.
That he wanted to put his own blazing mark among the stars,
And that it would shine so bright,
And float far above,
Far above
The quiet lake of the night.

Remember
by Evyn Czebiniak

Remember
When my time is over and I'm gone,
Remember Me,
When I'm not here and you are,
Remember Me,
Not with tears, not with a fall,
Remember Me,
Not through hurt, or pain, or fear,
Remember Me,
Not for what I did wrong,
Not for what I did right,
But for who I was,
Remember Me, As I Remember You,
Or don't Remember Me at all.

My World
by Deanna Binni-Bowers

My World is four girls
Maturing so fast,
changes that last
In my heart I still see,
the little baby staring at me
Sisters for life,
Even through pain and strife
We stick together through twists and twirls
Half-sisters or full
Push or pull
Night or day
Leave or stay
Love won't fail
We won't bail
Together we will pull through
Cause those girls are my crew

Suicide, Death By Shakespeare
by Lilly Keim

For who would bear the whips and scorns of time
If one could just end 'em now and be fine
Let long live all be hope and peace and trust
And you be first of that and more and just
I send my wish, for you. I call, I pray
I hope my words reach you, live long another day
Speak the Speak and Write what's wrote 'til Sunday's end
I wish the best. Don't end the best, my friend
Don't end thy life that God's given despair and strife
Stay dawn and stay with life. Oh, Please hear
My call. Let it reach to you and too, your-peers
Who walk the same trail as you before
I wish for none to take this trail no more
And, If you die, let not be thou in vain
Let you be last and end this deadly game.
I wish you luck for what comes next below
Or above and see the Gilded gates and go
I will see you, love, and soon again
And help many on that trail my friend
- Based on William Shakespeare's "Hamlet" as told by Horatio
What If Hamlet committed suicide?

#1
by Bridget Merkins

Everything's okay.
You're alright.
This is not your final day.
You will survive tonight.
They're laughing at you, you're just a joke, a punchline.
They see you as lesser, and smile when you whine.
You may be truly hurting.
It never gets old!
Everything's okay.
You're safe here.
This is not your final day.
You have nothing to fear.
Pain is humor.
Humor is pain.
You have nothing to lose.
And nothing to gain.
You're tired of lying.
Why are you trying?
They don't know that
Beneath the mask you're crying.

Blank Ovals
by Charlotte Hughes

You seem to think
I want a vote
a voice
a choice
a brain behind my grin
but all I want are blank ovals
and a sharpie to fill them in.
I'd color each
in orderly lines.
like soldiers
they smolder
a fire tinged vapor
but it won't burn away all my blank ovals
or the sharpie marks bleeding into the paper.
But no one gives any ovals to me
Just sharpie bruises of black and blue.
So if society ever lets me be free
I'll fill in an oval for you.

Descent
by Emma Reid

Twirling, dancing leaf
Drifting down in yellow sun
Calm, peaceful descent

Summer
by Sophia Wang

Crisp morning air by the
Early morning tide
Waves are high
Galloping through the sand
The big 'ole ball bouncing high and low
With us grinning through it all.
Knowing it's the last day of fun
When everyone's wearing white
The big 'ole ball still bouncing up and down,
But now we are saddened by the departure
Of the great glory of summer fun.

Sincerely, Rosaline
by Briana Boyer

To my Romeo,
I hope that you'll come soon
Lest I die
Before I am wed at dawn
Before my nightmare binds me
To his Juliet
I hope that he will find you
Lest you fall
For the man that watches you
Be wary, he is not true
To the poor Paris,
Who is watching from afar
I pray that harm befalls
Upon the man that sought you
True love binds, yet murder breaks

Dusk
by Lydia Wagner

Flowers close up shop
The land is splashed with black ink
Moon's light: milky white

Golden Hour
by Rhiannon Loudermilk

As the golden hour fades,
She allows the honey to suffocate her.
To flow is to solidify.
As to know her is to breath.
She must shift her weary soul.
Upon the flowing hour,
Time shall shift.

She
by Abby Powell

Worn down black Converse
and black jeans with rips in the knees.
Frizzy brown hair
and baggy t-shirts.
A laugh that fills an entire room
and a warm smile that's always plastered across her face.
The smallest things make her happy.
She loves sunsets
and dusk
whenever the air gets foggy and pink.
She cries when I cry because she hates seeing the people she loves sad
and she laughs when I laugh because she just can't help it.
She's quiet,
and thoughtful,
smart, and beautiful.
And she's kind to everyone
no matter what.

Vicissitude
by Jason Abreu

I think of her even when she is not;
neither roses or orchids can compare.
Then her petals begin to shed; A plot.
She splits my heart into two; a grand tear.
A profound feeling, much to my despair.
I would reminisce about the good times,
where I showed her my tender loving care.
It then took a turn for the worse; a crime.
Caught red-handed, a cheater, in her prime.
Do I pick myself up or do I feel?
At least I tried, she was busy; a mime.
Life is just a bipolar photo reel.
Do I take a chance on love; let it rot?
My heart is tangled in one big love knot.

The Smoking Orange
by Joshua Bauer

Every now and then
An orange will start to smoke
The tiny cells inside
Over time begin to choke
The fruit is left there helpless
Dying slowly in the sand
While the guiding force above
Says that all of it is planned
Its color turns to grey
And the orange is out of time
The darkness turns to day
And the sun begins to shine
The only thing remaining
Is a tiny little seed
Sitting lonely in the sand
But it finally was freed
Although it had potential
It would have to see through smoke
For the desert had surprises
As the little seed awoke

A Self-Destructive Therapy
by Kairi Hall

For eternity,
it seems
as if
i have been
wrenching
these words
out of
feelings
and nothings
until nothing
is all
that i am
feeling
anymore.
if this is poetry,
i don't want it.

Sisters
by Avigayil Resnick

Sisters are gifts given from Hashem,
Sisters are rings with a sparkling gem.
Sisters are the sunshine that brightens up a gloomy day,
Sisters are photos that never fade away.
Sisters are friendships, treasured forever,
Sisters are memories, always shared together.
Sisters are conversations that don't have an end,
Sisters are forgiving, they always make amends.
Sisters are hugs, always there to comfort you,
Sisters are the answer when you don't know what to do.
Sisters are cherries that may be apart,
Sisters are magnets, always close at heart.
Sisters are loving words that make a smile appear,
Sisters are tissues that wipe away the tears.
Sisters are sleepovers that are filled with fun,
Sisters are snow, reflecting against the sun.
Sisters are seeing eye dogs that guide you when you're lost,
Sisters are priceless, you can't buy them at any cost.

Infatuated
by Alyssa Jackler

Strand after strand falls,
And butterflies fill my stomach.
I'm certain it is as smooth as silk,
Even though I've never touched it.
Word after word cascades,
Every sentence is like a lullaby.
And whenever I hear the sound,
I feel as though I'm floating in the sky.
Giggle after giggle echoes,
My heart wishes to be closer.
However, I will just keep listening,
Replaying the melody over and over.
Thought after thought forms,
As my eyes gaze upon those lips.
Their rosy shade makes me blush,
Oh, watch me as I tip, tip, tip.

The True Victory
by Benjamin Salzer

We are Soldiers standing tall,
We will defend what's right,
To get freedom once and for all.
No matter how arduous the fight,
We stand rigid, the Shadow won't scathe us,
But he'll try to conquer us by Night.
The darkness fights strong and cruelly,
But no matter how strong his commando,
We will not surrender the call of duty.
Yet we will have no victory by the Sword,
There is no victory in fighting,
But only in the redeeming power of Jesus Christ, our Lord.
We are powerless without Him,
Without Him we do no good,
Until He fills our hearts to the brim.
Christ alone is the true achiever,
He died on the cross of Calvary and rose again,
Which is why I, myself, am a true believer.

Wonderful Things
by Mary Reduzzi

I count the lovely things about you on my hands and toes,
But there's only ten here, and ten there,
and there's more than twenty I know.
The sweetest things upon your face
like dimples and freckles and eyes,
For when I look in them the blue engulfs me,
like miles and miles of skies.
Your lovely bones carry warm, gentle skin,
A place I could spend forever, my wonderful garden.
Without these features you'd be but a name,
A colorless canvas washed away by the rain.

Today Is (Not) a Good Day
by Grace Mangis

Everyday is the absolute worst day ever.
And don't try to convince me that
There is always a way to be good again
Because, when you take a closer look,
The world is a really evil place
Even if
Some goodness does shine through once in a while
Happiness and hope don't last
And it's not true that
True happiness can sometimes be obtained
Only if one's surroundings are good
It's not true that good exists
I'm sure you can agree that
The reality
Creates
My attitude
It's all beyond my control
And you'll never in a million years hear me say that
Today was a good day

(now read bottom to top.)

It's Crazy To Think
by Allison Alvarez

There was a time I never even knew you
A time when you were just that kid
who sat next to me in seventh-grade science.
A time when I could never imagine you changing my life
but you did, you changed me.
You make me so happy,
everyone around me can see it.
My parents have noticed a change,
more smiles, more laughter.
No one else's words can impact me the way yours can.
Everything else can fail and
everything can go wrong
but then there's you.
When I see you I know that nothing else matters
because you're here with me and you're here for me
and I'm here for you no matter what.
Don't let one doubt cross your mind because I'm here.
I've tried to be there for so many people
then found out they don't need me,
they don't want me in their lives.
That's okay because I have you and you have me too.
For as long as we both see it through.
Thank you!

1ST PLACE

The Internet Age
by Victoria Sparks

No longer the age of innovation
No longer the age of brick and stone
This is the age of my phone screen
being the first welcoming face in the morning and the last laugh I take at night
This is the age of making fake accounts
to pretend you get as many likes as the next girl that shows up on your feed
The age where sitting together means everyone on a different app
on a different phone, so far away from each other it hurts
Let me tell you about this age
You'll know loneliness like the lines on your own hand,
but the tinder matches telling you are likable will keep you sane enough
You'll know insomnia like the road home,
because your mind won't be able to handle not being overstimulated
long enough for you to fall asleep at night
You'll know overthinking as if you invented it because screenshots and texts
and Instagram DM's mean that every word you send can last forever
No longer the age of the American dream
No longer the age of the cavemen
Just a dark room, the only light a dinging cellphone,
and you alone hoping it's not another streak snap
because God knows it's been awhile since you've talked to anyone

INDEX OF AUTHORS

★★★★★★★★

A

Abdulahad, Kyaijah 159
Abreu, Jason 196
Ackerman, Kristin 125
Adamczyk, Travis 47
Ahmad, Aaliah 146
Ahn, Lydia 72
Alexander, Aniyah 74
Allen, Michael 104
Alvarez, Allison 200
Amenuvor, Elikem 116
Anderson, Benjamin 29
Anderson, Natalia 122
Andrews, James 106
Angelo, Emily 56
Angelucci, Sarah 34
Angstadt, Macy 15
Aquilone, Mario 51
Arevalo-Lis, Isabella 92
Arriaga, Ashley M. 172
Arvas, Ayse 29
Astrow, Preston 165

B

Baker, Greenleebay 64
Banos, Estefania 49
Barletta, Ashley 190
Barone, Anthony 93
Barrows, Natalie 152
Battisti, Natalya 11
Batuyong, Lauren 71
Bauer, Joshua 196

Baunoch, Maizie 50
Beecher, Nathan 90
Beiler, Audrey 31
Beiler, Leona 135
Bellush, Natalie 147
Benitez, Alison 162
Bensley, Jennifer 93
Benson, Madalyn 126
Berresford, Ronae 21
Bigelow, Ainsley 113
Binni-Bowers, D. 192
Blackwell, Logan 67
Blasdell, Grace 23
Blocher, Kennedy 162
Boam, Gregory 60
Boland, Aiden 82
Bolkovich, Kiera 110
Bonnet, Hortense 67
Borrello, Reyna 109
Bowers, Luke 146
Boyer, Briana 194
Branch, Jada 24
Brandon, Miranda 165
Brandt, Antonia 37
Breakiron, Abigail 102
Brown, Abigail 165
Brown, Allaina 110
Brown, Jacob 73
Brugger, Graydon 60
Bryson, Keira 36
Buckley, Darragh 75
Buonagurio, Massimo 65
Buono, Valentina 36

Buscher, RJ 108
Butterfield, Tyler 147
Byers, Abby 78
Byler, Nathan 164

C

Calabrese, Jamie 56
Camacho, Daniel 96
Camacho, Haize 156
Canada, Bobby 99
Cariello, Julia M. 67
Carnahan, Serena 48
Carr, Olivia 45
Cauchi, Merrit 44
Chaklos, Annabella 141
Chapman, Cameron 95
Chelius, Megan 82
Christensen, Kira 177
Cirillo, Nicholas 36
Cizin, Sadie 108
Clendaniel, Shaeliyah 71
Clough, Maya 112
Clydesdale, Crystal 8
Cobb, Tori 77
Coles, Raymond 97
Collins, Alexa 130
Colón, Heaven 162
Comerate, Mary Teresa 186
Comerford, Sophie 32
Conklin, Emma 61
Contreras, Miley 129
Cook, Eliza 35
Cook, Parker 39

INDEX OF AUTHORS

Cook, Tyler 47
Copeland, Kaitlyn 163
Craig, Katherine 61
Crissy, Jayce 85
Crome, Simone 24
Crow, Brady 118
Crum, Olivia 136
Czebiniak, Ashlynn 25
Czebiniak, Eliyah 137
Czebiniak, Evyn 191
Czebiniak, Owen 187

D

DeChiaro, Michael 45
Deery, Desireé 189
Del Buono, Nicholas 133
Delgado, Julia 23
DeLuca, Taylor 157
DesJardins, Sean 72
DiBella, John C. III 188
DiFilippo, Haley 127
Dion, Emeli 183
DiPaolo, Cristina 21
Disant, Olivia 157
Dixon, Ava 83
Dorries, Graciana 172
Dragonetti, Alessia 26
Dugan, Kasey 75
Duncan, Delana 107
Duncan, Jaylee 109
Dyson, Lucia 20
Dzaferovic, Sara 36

E

Easter, Emma 149
Ebright, Isaac 59
Edlund, Sofia 142
Ehrgott, Zoai 134
Engels, Archer 41
Everett, Christopher 141

F

Fannon, Caroline 111
Farrell, Nicole 164
Feger, Emelia 30
Feiner, Niki 145
Ferguson, Morgan 178
Ferrari, Antonella 74
Ferretti, John 78
Fetter, Brett 92
Foose, Scotia 164
Fox, Austin 57
Frangione, Victoria 172
Frank, Norah 127
Fredericksdorf, R. 132
Freshwater, James 68
Fried, Gitty 101
Frushon, Haley 133

G

Galietta, Lily 100
Galizia, James 106
Gallo, Nicholas 143
Garner, Yvonne 21
Gebeloff, Harrison 32
Geniton, Savannah 31
Genus, Olivia 35
Ginsburg, Eli 85
Ginsburg, Eva 89
Giordano, Mario 191
Godek, Emily 8
Godzak, Isabella 76
Gonzalez, Gabriella 55
Gordon, Gabriella 73
Gorham, Conleth 143
Granger, Spencer 83
Grant, Lily 136
Grasso, Alyssa 155
Graziani, Arianna 122
Grimaldi, Joseph 139
Grinstead, Keira 77
Grodensky, Julia 104
Guadagnoli, Nellina 19
Gurango, Isabelle Rae 84

H

Haiyder, Mairaa 13
Hall, Kairi 197
Hamilton, Madelyn 112
Hara, Harper 32
Hardy, Michaela 29
Harris, Kensley 89
Harrison, Blaine 28
Harrison, Gabriella 91
Harrison, Sabrina 173
Hart, Kelsey 180
Hartmann, Rachel 158
Hartman-Vicinanza, J. 10
Hatfield, Blake 39
Heaton, Ava 91
Hechler, Quinn 81
Heckman, Kira 51
Herzog, Alivia 137
Higgins, Chauncey 176
Hillegas, Annabella 9
Hill, Madalynn 152
Hobbs, Julz 27
Hodge, Jaiden 175
Hogan, Fiona 188
Hollinger, Nicole 55
Hoover, Alissa 161
Horne, Isabella 8
Houle, Amber 171
Huang, Sarah 170
Hughes, Charlotte 193
Hulse, Olivia 59

I

Idioma, Claudia 125
Iglesias, Alex 101
Imbriano, Joe 111
Imperiale, Giacomo 92
Ince, Moriah 130
Inzerillo, Amanda 16
Ismail, Amira 127
Iyer, Anupama 54

INDEX OF AUTHORS

J

Jackler, Alyssa 198
Jackson, Alaina 9
Jacob, Azi 10
Janczuk, Monika 34
Jansen, Ava 134
Jefferson, Hannah 53
Jenkins, Josie 74
Jensen, Paige 83
John, Delia 46
Johnson, Adrianna 104
Johnson, Camille 27
Johnson, Cassandra 167
Johnson, Janiyah 64
Jones, Amanda 179
Jordan, James 64
Jose, Max 121
Juricek, Sheera 69

K

Kaiser, William 31
Katz, Chayalla 105
Kaur, Sukhpreet 146
Keene, Costello 156
Keim, Lilly 192
Kells, Mary Rose 11
Khan, Aaisha 62
Khanali, Samaya 145
Khandelwal, Anushka 171
King, Alyssa 190
King, Charlotte 116
Kioko, Sofia 86
Kipp, Anna 163
Klatzko, Zahava 117
Kodali, Anisha 121
Kossup, Sabrina 20
Kotten, Christian 159
Kovaleski, Lillian 37
Krithivasan, Nandini 120
Kruppa, Giovanni 136
Krwawicz, Jessica 68
Krwawicz, John 179
Kuhn, Clarissa 147

L

LaCoe, Jayden 185
Lall, Liana M. 15
Lambrianidis, Aidan 13
Lateer, Melody 169
Latimer, Brodie 16
Lavin, Madilyn 17
Lawrence, Matthew 27
Lawrence, Michelle 119
Lechner, Valentina 39
Lee, Alexander 187
Lee, Connor 99
Lestage, Jenna 167
Linares, Isabella 34
Lipari, Heather 184
Lipscomb, Joei 167
Llego, Justin 37
LoBue, Abigail 81
Locklear, Failyn 69
Longnecker, Amelia 80
Lopez, Andrea 77
Lopez, Sabrina 23
Lorenzo, Erik 109
Loudermilk, R. 195
Lustig, Ruby 80
Lyon, Claire 8

M

Macnow, Natalie 106
MacWilliams, B. 35
Makowka, David 91
Maksym, Isadora 186
Maliakal, Anna 66
Mangis, Grace 199
Marshall, Shane 160
Martinez, Angelina 53
Martinez, Margaret 66
Martori, Khloe 58
Mauceri, Olivia 38
Mayne, Nora 123
Mcalister, Calum 49
McAuley, James V 37

McCardell, Derek 175
McCommons, Lindsay 158
McCune, Alex 155
McFarland, Madison 168
McGoldrick, Kellen 24
McGovern, Corbi 140
McGowan, Milena 70
Mckeever, Leianna 166
McKenna, Luke 185
McLaughlin, Esme 66
McNall, Alexis 28
Mehta, Riyan 124
Mendes, Jasmin 140
Menter Jones, Elsa 128
Merkins, Bridget 193
Merlo, Sarah 44
Merriman-Mendez, F. 189
Messer, Hannah 187
Messina, Lanabelle 14
Mest, Peyton 82
Mikovich, Hannah 52
Miller, Jessie 178
Miller, Kelly 114
Miller, Kylie 57
Mirimanyan, George 69
Mitchell, Alana 96
Mitchell, Leisa 137
Mlyn, Sarah 118
Moore, Noah 31
Moore, Wendy 161
Morey, Emma 182
Morse, Alanna 160
Mullakandov, Gabriella 75
Murray, Brodie 40
Musto, Beatrice 111

N

Najim, Alinur 126
Najim, Rabiya 113
Nalepa, Agnieszka 44
Nichter, Alyssa 38
Nicotra, Cierra 25
Norelli, Benjamin 19

INDEX OF AUTHORS

Norelli, Lena 98
Nugent, Charles 14

O

Ochoa, Isabella 76
Olidge-Evans, Ethan 154
Orluk, Scarlett 63
Osborne, Madison 87
Osborne, Morgan 87
Osorio, Xavier Jonathan 11
Oswald, Emily 183

P

Pagliuca, Brianna 30
Pakan, Leah 88
Pandilwar, Vainavi 22
Panjwani, Imad 78
Paolillo, John 58
Paradiso, Alessandro 26
Parker, Will 59
Paskey, Elizabeth 124
Patti, Alessandra 84
Patton, Ireisha 139
Payne, Olivia 170
Peavy, Taylor 120
Peden, Abby 94
Pedroza, Karina 144
Perrie, Daniel 119
Persampire, Lyndsey 184
Peryea, Alex 107
Peterson, Jayla 107
Petri, Kate 139
Phelps, Willow 95
Phillips, Carson 79
Pickering, James 174
Piekarski, Natalia 45
Pillittere, Bella 105
Pirozzi, Joseph 33
Plaksienko, Nate 20
Polakovsky, Heidi 18
Polyansky, Alexander 123
Polycarpe, Julia 71
Potts, Julia 12
Powell, Abby 195
Praszkowicz, Sara 138
Prins, Channing 153

R

Race, Emma 170
Radinsky, Alexandra 128
Rafferty, Morgan 94
Rappoport, Rachel 46
Raymond, Caylin 25
Raza, Hafsah 93
Reduzzi, Mary 199
Regino, Jack 117
Reid, Brendan 70
Reid, Emma 194
Resnick, Avigayil 197
Riether, Sarah 54
Rivera, Ariana 153
Robert, Michael 58
Robinson, Jocelyn 58
Rodriguez, Aidan 79
Rodriguez, Cristopher 22
Roffman, Chava Rivka 10
Rosar, Alexandria 18
Rose, Katie 177
Rosenberg, Alice 50
Rosero, Sophia 9
Rossman, Anna 135
Rotos, Deanna 28
Roxburgh, Samantha 176
Rozario, Shreya 17
Russo, Jessica 56
Russo, Mary Kate 30
Russo, Steven 103

S

Sabo, Miah 102
Sackey, Samantya 182
Salzer, Benjamin 198
Scherer, Mason 130
Schmitt, Elise 181
Schumacher, Daniel, Jr. 15
Sclavunos, Justin 90
Sealey, Aryel 114
Setti, Rebekah 129
Settle, Ryan 88
Shahan, Lily 97
Shea, Grady 33
Sheahan, Katharine 132
Sheps, Michal 103
Sherman, E. 180
Shives, Logan 171
Shiv, Kanisha 12
Siabanis, George 11
Singh, Ajay 9
Singla, Krishav 52
Skelly, Aine 27
Skelly, Joseph 38
Smith, Amy 181
Smith, Jamie 86
Smith, Joey 40
Sniadach, Keeley 106
Snyder, Piper 60
Snyder, Zach 65
Solano, Nicolette 33
Somerville, Trista 45
Soneja, Pratham 17
Sottile, Annabella 115
Sparks, Victoria 201
Staudte, Ethan 186
Steeber, Sienna 80
Stetts, Sophie 131
St. Hilaire, Autumn 84
Stone, Cory 59
Storvig-Newson, A. 44
Strobel, Sienna 62
Stroup, Mitch 105
Suders, Bryce 168
Sundberg, Kyle 73
Sutowski, Kayla 35
Swiderski, Abigail 115

T

Takats, Jimmy 166
Talbott, Garrett 169
Tambone, Sophia 8

INDEX OF AUTHORS

Tejeda, Nicole 107
Terhune, Claire 126
Thompson, C. 154
Thompson, Gavin 70
Tone, Charlotte 16
Torrance, Regina 110
Torres, Mia Sara 131
Trejgis, Amelia 9
Turcot, Allyssa 144
Tweddle, Joshua 85
Tzagarakis, Ariana 30

U

Umar, Iman 48
Ureña, Malcolm 131

V

Vachino, Massimo 10
Valenti, Giovanni 79
Valentine, Simone 98
Vanasco, Tessa 19
VanKleek-Eagan, Timothy, Jr. 22
Vasquez, Juliana 18
Vetri, Madelyn 26
Vice, Olivia 173
Vidal, Hailey 26
Virgilio, Giuseppe 57
Virgil, Lucia 34
Vladimiroff, Lucas 163

W

Wadsworth, Alex 190
Wagner, Lydia 195
Walz, Lena 61
Wang, Sarah 14
Wang, Sophia 194
Ward, Jonathan 138
Washington-Patterson, Morgon 63
Whalen, Luke 65
Whetstone, Hailie 166
Whitney, Braden 81
Whyte, Mia 40
Wick, Gabrielle 174
Widmer, Marty 138
Widmer, Rosie 76
Williams, Alexandra 191
Willner, Chaya 148
Wright, Chloe 100

Y

Yakubov, Ethan 108
YounKin, Kearstin 142

Z

Zaccaria, Annelyse 68
Zdrojewski, Joshua 72
Zehner, Lauren 90
Zhang, Irina 173

2020 RISING STARS COLLECTION

Price List

Initial Copy 34.99

Additional Copies 26.00

Please Enclose $5 Shipping/Handling Each Order

Must specify book title and name of student author

Check or Money Order Payable to:

Appelley Publishing
P.O. Box 582
Tarpon Springs, FL 34688

Please Allow 4-8 Weeks For Delivery

www.appelley.org

Email: help@appelley.org